WE ONLY KNOW MEN

Patrick Henry

WE ONLY KNOW MEN

The Rescue of Jews in France
during the Holocaust

The Catholic University of America Press
Washington, D.C.

The paper used in this publication meets the minimum require-
ments of American National Standards for Information Science—
Permanence of Paper for Printed Library Materials, ANSI Z39.48-
1984.

∞

Library of Congress Cataloging-in-Publication Data

Henry, Patrick (Patrick Gerard)

We only know men : the rescue of Jews in France during the
Holocaust / Patrick Henry. — 1st ed.

p. cm.

Includes bibliographical references and index.

ISBN-13: 978-0-8132-1493-1 (cloth : alk. paper)

ISBN-10: 0-8132-1493-9 (cloth : alk. paper)

1. World War, 1939–1945—Jews—Rescue—France—
Le Chambon-sur-Lignon Region.   2. Holocaust, Jewish (1939–
1945)—France—Le Chambon-sur-Lignon Region—Biography.

3. Camus, Albert, 1913–1960. Peste.   4. World War, 1939–
1945—Jews—Rescue—Europe.   I. Title.

D810.J4H424 2007

940.53'18350944595—dc22

2006026499

We don't know what a Jew is, we only know men.

André Trocmé, August 1942

Contents

Illustrations

Foreword

It was most probably in the spring of 1988 when I first contacted Philip Hallie. I was beginning to think about editing a collection of essays on Montaigne.[1] Hallie was one of my favorite commentators on the *Essays* and I wanted him to write an article for the collection. He had published *The Scar of Montaigne,*[2] an insightful and important study of the essayist's irresolution, of his skepticism, and of the importance of experience in the *Essays*. More crucial still, for me, was Hallie's article entitled "The Ethics of Montaigne's 'Of Cruelty,'"[3] a groundbreaking analysis of the ethical revolution constituted by Montaigne's thought: a move away from concentration on the self in "egocentric" ethics toward the value of the deed itself and its consequences.

Hallie was much more than cordial. He seemed flattered to have been asked and genuinely happy to learn that someone he did not know three thousand miles away was interested not only in his work but much more importantly in the ethics of the *Essays*. Regarding the article for my collection, however, Hallie was not interested. Montaigne clearly remained his favorite philosopher, he said, but he had moved on to other things.

1. Patrick Henry, ed., *Approaches to Teaching Montaigne's "Essays"* (New York: Modern Language Association of America, 1994).

2. Philip Hallie, *The Scar of Montaigne* (Middletown, Conn.: Wesleyan University Press, 1966).

3. Philip Hallie, "The Ethics of Montaigne's 'De la cruauté,'" in *O un Amy! Essays on Montaigne in Honor of Donald M. Frame,* ed. Raymond La Charité (Lexington, Ky.: French Forum, 1977), 156–71.

"What other things?" I asked, not wanting to end the conversation abruptly simply because he had turned me down. He said he had published a book a decade earlier, entitled *Lest Innocent Blood Be Shed: The Story of the Village of Le Chambon and How Goodness Happened There*,[4] and had become tremendously interested in the rescuers of Jews in France during the Holocaust. He suggested that if I read the book and was interested in the ethical questions it raised, I should call Bill Moyers to ask him for a copy of the 1987 PBS video *Facing Evil*, in which Hallie appears and reflects upon the village eight years after publishing his study about the importance of what happened there.

I read the book, saw the PBS video and, while I continued to teach my courses on French literature of the Renaissance and the Enlightenment, began spending time each semester looking into the phenomenon of rescue in France during the Holocaust in the same area that Hallie had studied. Although I would never meet Philip Hallie, we talked often on the phone from 1988 until his death in 1994. His enthusiasm was as inextinguishable as it was contagious. Ethical principles were vital to him; he wore his on his sleeve. They were not simply to be contemplated in the abstract but rather worked through in the flesh. I invited him to speak at Whitman College, but he fell ill just before this engagement and was unable to make the trip. Although he never set foot on our campus, Hallie did make it to Whitman College: every graduating senior for one two-year period read *Lest Innocent Blood Be Shed* in our Senior Colloquium.

Almost twenty years after that first phone call to Hallie and twenty-eight years after the initial publication of *Lest Innocent Blood Be Shed*, I present here my own study on the rescuers. Work-

4. Philip Hallie, *Lest Innocent Blood Be Shed: The Story of the Village of Le Chambon and How Goodness Happened There* (1979; New York: Harper & Row, 1994). All future references are inserted parenthetically. While the pagination of the text is the same in both editions, the two have different prefaces. Page references to the preface therefore are preceded by the date of the edition to which they refer.

ing with documents, letters, and interviews unavailable to Hallie, I reconsider what took place on the plateau Vivarais-Lignon from 1939 to 1944 and examine in depth the research of the last quarter-century on Holocaust rescue in that area. This enables me to reevaluate the strengths and weaknesses of Hallie's groundbreaking study as they appear sixty-two years after the end of World War II. In addition, I look closely at the lives and work of two rescuers on the plateau, a young Protestant man, Daniel Trocmé, and a Jewish mother of three, Madeleine Dreyfus, both of whom were arrested and deported. Daniel died in the gas chamber at Maidanek; Madeleine survived Bergen-Belsen. This not uncommon example of a Jewish rescuer of Jews raises the issues of so-called Jewish passivity during the Holocaust and the lack of public recognition of Jewish rescuers of Jews. I also examine in detail Albert Camus' chronicle *The Plague,* written in large part during the fifteen months Camus spent in a hamlet just outside the village of Le Chambon-sur-Lignon from August 1942 until November 1943. As an allegorical mirror, the text reflects the violent and nonviolent resistance taking place when and where Camus composed his narrative. In the final chapter, I bring together my own findings and those of others who have studied the rescuers throughout Europe in order to show incontrovertibly why it is important not only to know about the victims and the perpetrators of the Nazi genocide but to study and to teach the rescuers of Jews during the Holocaust.

Acknowledgments

Philip Hallie is not the only one I am indebted to. Pierre Sauvage has created the only living monument to what happened on the plateau Vivarais-Lignon from 1939 to 1944: his beautifully constructed, award-winning, powerful documentary *Weapons of the Spirit.* Pierre's interviews with the rescuers are moving and essential to anyone who wants to know why and how this rescue activity took place. I quote these rescuers throughout my book. But watching them was just as important as listening to them. Their demeanor, modesty, simplicity, and serenity inspired me particularly in the writing of chapter 4. It was also in this film that I learned of the existence of Madeleine Dreyfus, who is never mentioned in Hallie's account. I should add too that there are a couple of indispensable quotations in my book, such as the title of the film, that I knew from the film before I found them later in my own research. Finally, at a conference in Minneapolis in the mid-1990s, Pierre did me the enormous favor of introducing me to Nelly Trocmé Hewett.

Nelly Trocmé Hewett, the daughter of André and Magda Trocmé, was a teenager in Le Chambon-sur-Lignon during World War II. She put me in touch with the family of Daniel Trocmé and numerous other people in France and Israel who played a role in this rescue activity and whom I cite in the following pages. She also gave me copies of the one thousand or so unpublished pages that constitute her parents' collective autobiographical papers, which have been invaluable to me in my work. She never tried to influence my views on the World War II history of the plateau Vivarais-Lignon.

Nelly Trocmé Hewett introduced me to Annik Flaud, an independent researcher in Le Chambon-sur-Lignon who knows more about the plateau and its history than anyone else I've worked with. Annik put me in contact with the family of Madeleine Dreyfus, secured documents, checked dozens of references, and generously shared her vast knowledge with me. She also drove me to all the places I write about on the plateau and introduced me to several people who lived there during the war. As the footnotes indicate, Annik was crucial in the writing of this book.

I am indebted to Robert Trocmé, who gave me copies of his brother Daniel's letters to his parents from September 11, 1942, to February 6, 1944, and other unpublished family documents, without which I could not have written chapter 2. I am equally beholden to Michel Dreyfus, the son of Madeleine Dreyfus, who patiently found answers to all my questions about his mother and sent me a large box full of unpublished letters, documents, and academic talks and papers all written by his mother, and memoirs written by both his parents, himself, and his sister, Annette Davis. Naturally, I could not have written chapter 3 without them. I am deeply saddened by the fact that Michel died before this book appeared in print. I remember his warmth, sense of humor, generosity, and gratitude when I met him for the only time in his hospital room in Paris. May his memory be a blessing.

I am also grateful to Claudine Salamon, archivist at Oeuvre de secours aux enfants in Paris, who forwarded useful documents to me concerning Madeleine Dreyfus and OSE; three women who were involved in different forms of resistance in France and were kind enough to respond to my queries: Vivette Samuel, Denise Siekierski, and especially Lili-Elise Garel, who was arrested at the same time as Madeleine Dreyfus; and André Chouraqui, who knew Albert Camus in Algeria and on the plateau Vivarais-Lignon, and responded immediately every time I sent him questions regarding Camus' presence in the area of Le Chambon-sur-Lignon.

Closer to home, from the very beginning, I had Sandy Goodhart, Ted Stein, Richard Kaplan, and Elliott Abramson for inspiration and encouragement. I am also grateful to Ted Stein and Russell McCormmach for reading earlier drafts of my book and for making important suggestions. I also want to thank Sandy Goodhart for inviting me twice to Purdue University to speak about my research; Berel Lang for his illuminating writings on ethics and stimulating and challenging conversations about the Holocaust and ethics; Richard Watson for his *tabula rasa* reading of the final draft; and Susan Suleiman for her many illuminating suggestions regarding the final content and structure of my text.

The road from the Renaissance to the Holocaust was also made smooth by Susan Suleiman's learned and engaging National Endowment for the Humanities seminar "War and Memory: Postwar Representations of the Occupation and World War II in French Literature, History, and Film" (Harvard University, summer 2000) and by the two-week Holocaust "Boot Camp" run by Zev Weiss and Peter Hayes at Northwestern University's Institute on the Holocaust and Jewish Civilization (summer 2003). I am also grateful to the Camargo Foundation in Cassis, France, where I was a resident fellow from January to June 1995. Although I went there to work on Montaigne (and did so), I also did research on the rescue of Jews in the south of France and visited the plateau Vivarais-Lignon several times. I thank the Washington Commission for the Humanities, and Linda Capell in particular, for sponsoring my lecture on the rescuers of Jews in the south of France, which I gave throughout the state of Washington from July 1996 to July 1998; and Stanlee Stahl for naming me, in 2000, one of the speakers for the Jewish Foundation for the Righteous in New York City (www.jfr.org). I am honored to be part of this wonderful organization. Kristin Vining-Stauffer has prepared the various drafts of this book with intelligence, patience, flexibility, goodwill, and creativity. I could not be more grateful for her assistance.

For various reasons, I also want to thank the following people:

Acknowledgments

Barbara Barnett, Lawrence Baron, Nathan Bracher, Jolene Chu, John Compton, Joe Corvino, John Desmond, Bob Ericksen, Eva Fogelman, Rosalie Footnick, Tess Gallagher, Myrna Goldenberg, Martin Goldman, Dan Gordon, Leonard Grob, (the late) Doris Hallie, Susan Healy, John Hill, Robert Johnson, Nancy Lefenfeld, René Lichtman, Joe Maier, Maurice Monier, Bob Moss, Larry Mulkerin, Bernard Otterman, Steve Rendall, Carol Rittner, Irving Roth, Irena Polkowska Rutenberg, Stephanie Seltzer, (the late) Roger Shattuck, Simon Sibelman, and Ken Waltzer. At the Catholic University of America Press, I am particularly indebted to Theresa Walker, Beth Benevides, and, once again, David McGonagle for his interest in my work, his fairness, and his patience. I would also like to thank Ellen Coughlin for doing a superb job of copyediting the manuscript and Denise Carlson for compiling the index.

There is no way I can adequately thank Mary Anne O'Neil, who has been my companion for the past thirty-four years. She is my best friend, my best reader, the source of most of my best inspiration, and the one with whom, on our daily four-mile walks, I have discussed most thoroughly all of the issues in this book. She's "the other half of what I am," "the missing piece," and all the other things that Bob Dylan chants in "Wedding Song." I'd be lost without her on paper and everywhere else.

Earlier, less-developed drafts of chapters 2, 3, and 4 appeared respectively as "Daniel's Choice: Daniel Trocmé (1912–1944)" in *The French Review* (March 2001), "Madeleine Dreyfus, Jewish Activity, Righteous Jews" in *Logos: A Journal of Catholic Thought and Culture* (Winter 2004), and "Albert Camus, Panelier, and *La Peste*" in *Literary Imagination: The Review of the Association of Literary Scholars and Critics* (Fall 2003). The author wishes to thank the editors of those journals for permission to reprint these pages. He is also grateful to the Swarthmore College Peace Collection for permission to quote from the papers of André and Magda Trocmé.

Preface

On June 23, 1940, a day after the armistice was signed between Germany and France, Pastors André Trocmé and Edouard Theis entered the pulpit of their church in Le Chambon-sur-Lignon and delivered a ringing sermon. They underscored the anti-Christian nature of Nazi doctrine and exhorted their parishioners to resist any orders that violated the teachings of the Gospels. "The duty of Christians," they insisted, "is to use the weapons of the Spirit to resist the violence that will be brought to bear on their consciences."[1] Christians were to resist "without fear, but also without pride and without hatred."

Despite the Nazi takeover of France, these pacifist Protestant leaders made it clear that all was not lost: "Faith has not been lost . . . the Gospel truths have not been lost . . . the Word of God has not been lost and that is where we find all the promises and possibilities of recovery for ourselves and our Church." The pastors urged their parishioners not to blame others for the current situation: "Everyone is accusing everyone else; everyone is trying to evade their own responsibilities by blaming one's fellow citizens or foreign peoples."

They proposed an end to all factions among people and a return to the values of early Christianity: "Today, let us abandon all divisions among Christians, all quarrels among French people. Let us

1. Edouard Theis and André Trocmé, "Message des deux pasteurs du Chambon à leur paroisse," *Le Plateau Vivarais-Lignon: Accueil et Résistance 1939–1944*, ed. Pierre Bolle et al. (Le Chambon-sur-Lignon: Société d'Histoire de la Montagne, 1992), 597–99. Unless otherwise noted, all translations from French to English in this book are mine.

stop labeling each other, designating one another in scornful terms
. . . Let us begin to have confidence in each other again, to greet and
welcome one another, recalling at each encounter, as did the first
Christians, that we are all brothers and sisters in Jesus Christ." This
message was taken to heart by the inhabitants of the entire plateau
Vivarais-Lignon who, over the following four years, sheltered several thousand mostly Jewish refugees.

Sixty-four years later, on July 8, 2004, President Jacques Chirac
came to Le Chambon-sur-Lignon to deliver an anti-racism speech
to the French nation. Racist attacks in France, principally but not
exclusively on Jews and Muslims, had increased alarmingly over
the prior two years and were now escalating even more. In 2003,
127 anti-Semitic acts were reported in France; during the first six
months of 2004, 135 anti-Semitic acts had already been noted.[2] In
addition, 207 racist acts that were not anti-Semitic, mostly perpe-
trated against Muslims, had taken place between January and May
2004, as opposed to 128 during the same period in 2003.[3] Both
Jewish and Muslim tombstones had recently been desecrated in
various cities in France.[4]

Chirac began by citing the important history of the plateau as a
sanctuary for persecuted people, which, during the Vichy regime, became "the moral conscience of our country," the place where, "when
put to the test, the soul of the nation affirmed itself."[5] The president
of the republic stressed how the people of the plateau had practiced
the principles that unite all French people, the values upon which
the nation was founded: "courage, generosity, dignity, tolerance, solidarity, and fraternity." Now, at a time when "odious and contempt-
ible acts of hatred are corrupting our country . . . endangering our
schools . . . menacing our children . . . profaning our places of wor-

2. Alain Genestar, "Casser la figure au racisme," *Paris Match*, July 15–21, 2004, 23.
3. *Libération*, July 9, 2004, 2.
4. Craig S. Smith, "Thwarted in Germany, Neo-Nazis Take Fascism to France,"
New York Times, August 13, 2004.
5. *L'Eveil* (a newspaper in the Haute Loire), July 9, 2004, 10. The entire speech
is on this page.

ship and our grave sites . . . affecting, in reality, all of our compatriots," Chirac urged the French nation, individually and collectively, to
avoid all passivity regarding racism against all groups, specifically referring to the racism against Jews, Muslims, and homosexuals.

Whereas Trocmé and Theis offered a unified vision of "brothers
and sisters in Jesus Christ," Chirac spoke movingly of a nation collectively opposed to hate crimes and bound together against racism:

> Such is the France I believe in: a France capable of the best, faith-
> ful to its history, its roots, its culture; an audacious France, a France
> committed to solidarity; a France that overcomes its fears and tran-
> scends itself in its effort to come to the aid of all those who need her
> help, protection, and support; a generous France that refuses ego-
> centrism, inward withdrawal, exclusions and discrimination; an open
> and welcoming France, united in its diversity and bearing with pride
> its ideal of justice and peace in Europe and in the world.

Chirac underscored the fact that the struggle for tolerance is "a fragile and never-ending conquest" at the same time that he assured
the nation that "crimes born of fanaticism, the desire to humiliate
. . . [and] the refusal to accept difference" would in all cases be punished to the full extent of the law.

In comparing the sermon by Trocmé and Theis to the speech by
Chirac, one must consider both continuity and change. Trocmé and
Theis stress the values of tolerance and unity in religious human-
ism. Chirac appeals to a secularism, based on those same humanis-
tic values of tolerance and solidarity, that "allows everyone to live
and practice their religion in perfect safety." While each discourse
is a clear and vivid call to action, Trocmé and Theis gave a sermon
in their church, Chirac a speech in the schoolyard across from the
church. Nonetheless, standing in that schoolyard, upholding human-
istic values in defense of the secular state, Chirac was offering a la-
icized version of the June 23, 1940, sermon by Trocmé and Theis.[6]

6. At the Memorial of the Shoah in Paris, President Chirac took advantage of the
sixtieth anniversary of the liberation of Auschwitz (January 25, 2005) to continue his

By choosing to give his anti-racist address in Le Chambon-sur-Lignon, Chirac marked the plateau as a powerful site of memory (*"lieu de mémoire,"* the term he himself used), a place which, during World War II, in the words of the president of the republic, "magnified the stature of France." During the Holocaust, the behavior of the people of the plateau Vivarais-Lignon was an exception. Sixty years later, President Chirac has designated it as an example of what multicultural France can and should be in the twenty-first century. "The example of the 'Plateau,'" he said, "shows us that the commitment of each one and the solidarity of everyone, day after day, constitute the strength and provide an example for all human communities." In welcoming President Chirac to the plateau, Francis Valla, the mayor of Le Chambon-sur-Lignon, expressed pride that the plateau could serve in such a capacity: "Our country, experiencing a period marked by outbursts of intolerance and inward withdrawal, needs some beacons in the night. Your presence at our side today is a way of telling us that the plateau Vivarais-Lignon might be one of those beacons."[7] For the plateau to serve as that model, however, the legends and myths that have been constructed about it have to be destroyed and what in fact really happened there from 1939 to 1944, and why, must be established. In addition to highlighting the importance and personalities of rescuers themselves, that is the main purpose of the text that follows.

---

fight against racism in France. "Anti-Semitism has no place in France," he said. "Anti-Semitism is not an opinion. It's a perversion. A perversion that kills." He recalled "the most somber hours of our history" and urged the French nation to "remain faithful to the humanist heritage that it then betrayed." "Chirac: l'antisémitisme 'n'a pas sa place en France,'" *France-Amérique,* January 29–February 4, 2005, 11. Once again, on April 24, 2005, the National Day of Remembrance of the Victims and Heroes of the Deportation, Chirac urged all French people "to fight without mercy against all forms of racism and antisemitism, all forms of revisionism, and against all those who proclaim a fundamental inequality among human beings." *Yahoo! Actualités-France,* April 24, 2005.

7. Francis Valla, "Monsieur le Président de la République, Mesdames, Messieurs," e-mail message from Annik Flaud (August 2, 2004).

WE ONLY KNOW MEN

1 ⌣⌣

Rescuing Jews in the
South of France

There are stars whose radiance is visible on earth though they have long been extinct. There are people whose [goodness] continues to light the world though they are no longer among the living. These lights are particularly bright when the night is dark.

Hannah Senesh[1]

How French people acted and reacted during the 1940–44 German Occupation of France has been the subject of fierce, diverse, and radically conflicting debates from the very first day after the German Army exited the country.[2] One might even claim that the myth of a united French resistance, later ironically dubbed *Résistancialisme,* began with de Gaulle's June 18, 1940, BBC speech urging the French not to give up in their struggle against the occupier and included, dramatically, at the moment of the liberation, his Au-

1. Hannah Senesh, *Hannah Senesh: Her Life and Diary* (New York: Schocken Books, 1972), 13.

2. On the myth of *Résistancialisme* and on the degrees of collaboration, accommodation, adaptation, and general *débrouillardise,* see the following three comprehensive and illuminating studies: Philippe Burrin, *France Under the Germans: Collaboration and Compromise,* trans. Janet Lloyd (New York: The New Press, 1996); Robert Gildea, *Marianne in Chains: Daily Life in the Heart of France During the German Occupation* (New York: Henry Holt and Company, 2002); Julian Jackson, *France: The Dark Years 1940–1944* (New York: Oxford University Press, 2001).

gust 25, 1944, march down the Champs-Elysées. In any event, in an attempt to unify a terribly fragmented postwar population and to restore its dignity and integrity, de Gaulle promulgated the myth that France had resisted the occupier and had liberated itself. Even if only a small minority had actually done the fighting, so went the myth, all Frenchmen, *la France éternelle*, in their collective dedication to freedom, supported the Resistance. This is a myth that the French were happy to accept.

With de Gaulle back in power in the 1960s, this myth reached its zenith, emblematically highlighted in 1964 when the general had the remains of the legendary Resistance hero Jean Moulin transferred to the Panthéon. That same year, the Resistance historian Henri Michel published his biography of Moulin. In 1969, Jean-Pierre Melville followed his earlier *Le Silence de la mer* (1947), a film about individual, isolated, passive, and silent resistance to the occupier, with a second film, entitled *L'Armée des ombres*, which presented an epic view of the struggles of the Resistance. This myth located "true France" in the Resistance, which had been generated by *la France éternelle*. Within *Résistancialisme*, therefore, there is a clear distinction between Vichy and the French state. As Julien Jackson points out in his masterful synthesis of the period, *France: The Dark Years 1940–1944*, while the Gaullists and Communists argued throughout the 1960s over who played the greater role in the Resistance, "the history of Vichy was largely ignored."[3]

This absence of critical scrutiny of Vichy ended abruptly at the beginning of the 1970s when the myth of *Résistancialisme* came tumbling down. Marcel Ophüls's 260-minute documentary, *Le Chagrin et la pitié*, released in 1971 but not shown on French television until 1981, pretty much ignored de Gaulle, emphasized collaboration as well as resistance, and depicted the majority of the nation as more or less indifferent to the horrors going on around them. While it did not in fact create a countermyth whereby all Frenchmen, ex-

3. Jackson, *France: The Dark Years*, 8–9.

cept for a few resisters, were collaborators, it was interpreted as having done so. Then in 1972, Robert O. Paxton's *Vichy France: Old Guard and New Order*, which was published in French in 1973, documented the active and vigorous collaboration of the Vichy leaders with Germany and delineated the specific agendas of Vichy itself, one of which was collaboration with the deportation of Jews from France. Paxton's seminal work, which thirty-five years later is still the best study of the Vichy regime, paints the French themselves, in a book that focuses on the government, as passively collaborating. Finally, in 1974, the film *Lacombe Lucien* appeared. Directed by Louis Malle from the screenplay by the novelist Patrick Modiano, this disturbing film displays the murky nature of the Occupation and depicts the links between collaboration and criminality.

In short, the myth of resistance was unexpectedly and completely shattered. France was now seen, not as a nation of resisters, but as a nation of collaborators. The French were forced to look at themselves in an unflattering mirror that reflected collaboration and self-interest at every level. In particular, the ultranegative view of Vichy established itself and developed in part because of a new Jewish self-consciousness, an attention to Jewish memory that continued unabated and, among many other manifestations, produced the greatest Holocaust documentary of all, *Shoah,* directed by Claude Lanzmann in 1985. An extraordinary output of books, articles, and films that deal with the Occupation years began to appear in the mid-1970s and continue to appear into the new century, all giving the lie to the still popular notion that France refuses to examine its 1940–44 history. On the contrary, even in 2007, the evils of Vichy are still a national obsession.

Beginning in the mid-1980s, scholars began to study French society of the years 1940–44, rather than simply the workings of the Vichy government. It soon became apparent that the idea of a "nation of collaborators" was as simplistic and reductive as that of a "nation of resisters." Each myth magnified a reality, resistance and collaboration, but left the overwhelming majority of the population out of the picture, for only a small percentage of people had been actively involved in either political collaboration or organized resistance.

Philippe Burrin's *France under the Germans: Collaboration and Compromise* and Robert Gildea's *Marianne in Chains: Daily Life in the Heart of France during the German Occupation* present a nuanced and convincing picture of French society during the years 1940–44. Burrin's widely and deeply informed analysis documents both organized resistance and active collaboration in a politico-ideological sense but presents the great majority of the French as accommodators, *attentistes,* and adapters whose sole desire was "to get through it." He acknowledges that "collaboration" was the most obvious manifestation of accommodation. Vichy was not dilatory in carrying out the Nazis' program and sometimes even anticipated it. He also examines other examples of "opportunistic accommodation" that he considers "collaboration." But not all forms of accommodation (establishing public services, creating a working economy, seeking out survival needs for one's family) can be called collaboration. Burrin sorts out the moral categorizations of individual acts on the accommodation spectrum.

Burrin finds that Vichy's politics were supported by a small minority and that support was "fragile, shaky, and dwindling." Until mid-1942, he claims, one-sixth to one-fifth of French people favored collaboration. But many did so out of expedience, with suspicion and resignation. This did not mean, however, that the others favored resistance, even after mid-1942 when support for Vichy fell drastically. Burrin concludes that "the great majority of French people had no faith in collaboration and wanted none of it . . . they did behave worthily, even if their uncertainty and passivity in the first two years allowed a certain latitude to those who were venturing further towards accommodation . . . To be a hero is honorable; not to be one is not necessarily dishonorable."[4]

4. Burrin, *France under the Germans,* 185; 183; 463–64.

Whereas Burrin concentrates on high politics, big business, lead-ing intellectuals, professional people, and publishers, Gildea writes about ordinary people hailing from *la France profonde*. He analyz-es workers, peasants, manufacturers, landowners, women, children, Catholics, and Jews in the Loire Valley. Like Burrin, Gildea writes "to break out of the straitjacket of interpretations based on the Resis-tance/collaboration version of events, while also refusing to reduce the French to passive victims of the Occupation, cold, hungry, and fearful."[5] Again, like Burrin, having discarded an overall Manichean view of things, Gildea sets up a more credible grey zone, focuses on strategies adopted and networks created, examines what was and was not considered acceptable behavior in the ambiguous moral uni-verse of the Occupation, and finds that the great majority were just trying to survive as best they could in cohabitation with the occupi-ers. "What is most striking about the French under the Occupation," he writes, "is not how heroic or villainous they were but how imagi-native, creative, and resourceful they were in pursuit of a better life."[6]

Only by comprehending the complex grey zone in France as a whole during the Occupation can one make sense of the confusing and contradictory puzzle that historians, novelists, and filmmakers have tried to solve. Gildea concludes that Franco-German relations were not always as brutal as they are regularly portrayed; and de-spite the repressive policies of Vichy and the Germans, at least the façade of a civil society remained, with the arts, theater, cinema, sports, and an upsurge in religious activities. While a very small mi-nority resisted and another small minority actively collaborated, the great majority of the French sought survival during an extraor-dinarily troubled and difficult time when, as Eugen Weber points out, "The caloric intake of the French may have been the lowest in Europe, less than half what it had been before the war."[7] In *Occupa-*

5. Gildea, *Marianne in Chains*, 403.
6. Ibid., 16.
7. Eugen Weber, "France's Downfall," *The Atlantic Monthly*, October 2001, 121.

tion: The Ordeal of France 1940–1944, Ian Ousby speaks of what the French call *la débrouillardise.* When seen in a positive light, this connotes an "admirable resourcefulness"; when perceived negatively, it suggests the ability to "accommodate oneself to officialdom." Ousby explains that the slang expression *le système D,* refers to *la débrouillardise* and concludes that "the Occupation was the golden age of *le système D.*"[8]

The preceding, prefatory, evolving critical overview of France during the Occupation will serve in many ways as a point of comparison as we examine and define the World War II legacy of Le Chambon-sur-Lignon and the plateau Vivarais-Lignon. From 1940 to 1944 on this plateau in south-central France, several thousand relatively isolated mountain people risked their lives and, in some cases, those of their children by sheltering thousands of refugees from the Nazis and the French police. Most of the refugees were Jewish and a large number of them were children. No other communal effort on this scale occurred for this length of time anywhere else in Occupied Europe. The groundbreaking study of this rescue mission is Philip Hallie's *Lest Innocent Blood Be Shed.* Hallie's book, however, has been severely criticized because of factual errors, historical inaccuracies, and various lacunae in its account. But Hallie never saw himself as a historian: "I knew that I could not tell the story," he writes in the original "prelude" to his book, "as thoroughly as a careful historian might tell it" [1979; p. 7]. Hallie wrote as a moral philosopher trying to grasp the phenomenon of nonviolence and the ethics of rescue in Nazi-dominated France. In writing about how goodness happened in the midst of evil, Hallie was a pioneer. Very little was known about the rescuers at the time he did his research and writing. Like most Holocaust survivors, the rescuers had not yet come forward to tell their stories. For one thing, most of

8. Ian Ousby, *Occupation: The Ordeal of France 1940–1944* (New York: St. Martin's Press, 1998), 125–26.

them did not think they had done anything exceptional. As a result, Hallie was exploring uncharted waters.[9]

While the moral evaluations in Hallie's narration are unassailable, it is unfortunate that he concentrated solely on André Trocmé and the village of Le Chambon-sur-Lignon.[10] By focusing on one village and a few important people therein (André Trocmé, Magda Trocmé, co-pastor Edouard Theis), Hallie unwittingly gives the erroneous impression that other people, pastors, and villages were not also at the heart of the rescue mission. Just as many camp survivors did not come forth until the Holocaust deniers had spoken, so too many of the rescuers in this area did not speak of what they had done until it was implied that they had done nothing. A three-day colloquium held in Le Chambon-sur-Lignon in October 1990 underscored a forty-five-year silence by the people on the plateau Vivarais-Lignon regarding rescue efforts during World War II. Speakers alluded to the *"Chambonisation"* of the phenomenon of rescue in this geographical area and worked to set the record straight a half-century after the events in question.[11]

Despite the historical and geographical limitations of Hallie's study, it is a brilliant analysis of the ethics of rescue, exactly as its

9. There is, however, no justification whatsoever for the absurd suggestion that the goal of Hallie's book is "to promote the thesis that Christian nonviolence is the only efficacious weapon against totalitarianism." Serge Bernard, "Territoire et marquage identitaire, haut Vivarais et haut Velay," in *La Deuxième Guerre mondiale, des terres de refuge aux musées,* ed. Patrick Cabanel and Laurent Gervereau (Le Chambon-sur-Lignon: Sivom Vivarais-Lignon, 2003), 100. See also Jacques Poujol, *Protestants dans la France en guerre 1939–1945. Dictionnaire thématique et biographique* (Paris: Les Editions de Paris, 2000), 138.

10. Hallie also singles out Major Julius Schmähling as someone who protected the village of Le Chambon-sur-Lignon from attacks by German forces in the area. Given the fact that both Jews and non-Jews died as a result of roundups in the village, many local people and others have voiced serious opposition to this claim. See, for example, Magda Trocmé, Madeleine Barot, Pierre Fayol, and O. Rosowsky, "Le Mythe du commandant SS protecteur des Juifs," *Le Monde Juif,* April–June 1988, 61–69.

11. Pierre Bolle et al., eds., *Le Plateau Vivarais-Lignon,* passim for references to the *Chambonisation* of the phenomenon of rescue on the plateau and to Major Schmähling.

author had intended. Hallie's pioneering study also brought international attention to the phenomenon of nonviolent resistance against the Nazis. As such, and given the fact that it was among the earliest and most widely read books about rescue, it unquestionably played a significant part in the collective determination to give a central role to nonviolent resistance in Holocaust museums throughout the world.

The 700-page volume containing the proceedings of the three-day 1990 colloquium held in Le Chambon-sur-Lignon constitutes our greatest single source of knowledge regarding the extent and nature of rescue work on the plateau. Although many issues, including statistical ones such as the number of refugees hidden on the plateau, have yet to be resolved and may never be resolved, this volume is our best source for moving beyond the legends into a true history of the plateau from 1939 to 1944. It is important that issues were faced squarely at the colloquium and that the editor, Pierre Bolle, recorded the debates as well as the papers delivered. It is equally important that we now attempt collectively to write as objective a history as possible in terms of both violent and nonviolent resistance against the Nazis and Vichy on the plateau Vivarais-Lignon while some of the witnesses and participants of that history are still alive to share their memories with us. While fully acknowledging the collective contributions of people across the plateau, my basic interest in the moral dimension of this rescue work has led me to concentrate mainly but not exclusively on nonviolent resistance in and around the village of Le Chambon-sur-Lignon.

As is indicated by the title of the volume of the proceedings of the 1990 colloquium, *Le Plateau Vivarais-Lignon: Accueil et Résistance 1939–1944,* the entire plateau contributed to the rescue of the refugees during the years of the Occupation. Ministers, policemen, farmers, shopkeepers, field workers, and people of all social classes participated in the sheltering and rescue work. This was acknowledged by the Jews rescued on the plateau who placed a plaque

Engraved stone in Yad Vashem in Jerusalem recognizing the people of the Plateau Vivarais-Lignon. It reads: "And your people, all of them, are righteous." Isaiah 60:21; "To the people of Le Chambon-sur-Lignon and the neighboring villages who saved the lives of a great number of Jewish people." *Photograph by Richard Deats, Fellowship of Reconciliation. Courtesy of Nelly Trocmé Hewett.*

in 1979 in the square across the street from the Protestant church in Le Chambon-sur-Lignon that reads: "Praise to the Protestant community of this Cévenol land and to all those led by its example, believers of all faiths and non-believers who, from 1939 to 1945, uniting together against the crimes of the Nazis, at the risk of their lives, during the Occupation, hid, protected, and saved thousands of those persecuted." Yad Vashem, the Holocaust Martyrs' and Heroes' Remembrance Authority in Jerusalem, awarded dozens of Righteous Gentile medals to individual people living on the plateau and also offered homage and the title of "righteous" to the people of the plateau in general. Situated in a small garden, the Yad Vashem plaque reads: "And your people, all of them, are righteous." Isaiah 60:21. "To the people of Le Chambon-sur-Lignon and the neighboring villages who saved the lives of a great number of Jewish people."

The Protestant pastors André Trocmé and Edouard Theis were the catalysts for much of what happened in and around the village

Plaque placed in 1979 in the square across the street from the Protestant church in Le Chambon-sur-Lignon. It reads: "The memory of the righteous will remain forever." Psalm 112. "Praise to the Protestant community of this Cévenol land and to all those led by its example, believers of all faiths and non-believers who, from 1939 to 1945, uniting together against the crimes of the Nazis, at the risk of their lives, during the Occupation, hid, protected and saved thousands of those persecuted." *Photograph by Patrick Henry.*

of Le Chambon-sur-Lignon between 1940 and 1944, but the rescue mission was a collective effort that involved not only thirteen other Protestant ministers and their followers in all twelve Protestant parishes on the plateau, but also Darbyites, Catholics, Swiss Protestants, American Quakers, Evangelicals, Jewish organizations such as Oeuvre de secours aux enfants (Children's Rescue Network, OSE), other organizations such as La Cimade and Secours suisse aux enfants, nonbelievers, students, Boy Scouts, underground railroad workers, farmers, city people themselves refugees, and other people from all walks of life. To a large degree, it was an ecumenical effort uniting Catholics, Protestants of many denominations, and Jews in a collective struggle against a powerful common enemy. No similar ecumenical endeavor has ever been undertaken on French soil.

Because the rescue operations included non-Protestants and nonbelievers, in 1979 the pastor in Le Chambon-sur-Lignon and his presbyterial council decided not to affix the plaque on the wall of the Protestant church but rather on a municipal building.[12] In a recent letter, Olivier Hatzfeld, a young historian in hiding who taught at the Ecole Nouvelle Cévenole in Le Chambon-sur-Lignon from 1942 to 1944, captures the remarkable solidarity on the plateau at the time that seemed to unite, beyond religious convictions, all those who believed in the human dignity of all individuals: "The first word that comes to mind when I try to express what we felt . . . in Le Chambon-sur-Lignon, is solidarity among everyone, longtime Chambonnais, yearly tourists, families looking for refuge, . . . students, teachers, shopkeepers, farmers."[13] This same solidarity existed across the plateau, where refugees were absorbed into the communal life and where not a single refugee was ever betrayed.

The collective nonviolent rescue mission on the plateau was truly remarkable. This is why Yad Vashem decided to honor the people of the plateau collectively as well as individually. It would have been impossible to find out the names of all the people who helped in the area, but by bestowing honor communally Yad Vashem would publicly recognize everyone who had helped in any way, even if not mentioned by name. In this regard, Le Chambon-sur-Lignon researcher Annik Flaud remarks: "This corresponds exactly to what the people on the plateau expected: collective recognition, not just individual recognition, for their parents' actions."[14]

This rescue mission took place in a Europe where, generally speaking, the gates of compassion for Jews were locked. Most people looked the other way or actively collaborated with the Nazis. Except in Denmark and Bulgaria, most churches remained silent. An

12. E-mail from Le Chambon-sur-Lignon researcher Annik Flaud to author, December 1, 2003.
13. Letter of September 13, 2003, from Olivier Hatzfeld to Patrick Cabanel. A copy of this letter is in my possession.
14. E-mail from Annik Flaud to author, December 2, 2003.

immense bureaucracy, in the tens of thousands, from local police and railroad clerks to lawyers, soldiers, and physicians, was involved in the rounding up, transportation, confinement, registration, deportation, and extermination of, among others, six million Jews— two-thirds of European Jewry.

This rescue mission occurred, too, not in a country like Denmark, where it was *not* a crime to hide a Jew and where 93 percent of the Jewish population was saved, but in France, whose Vichy government created a climate of extensive collaboration and accommodation with the Germans and where anti-Semitism and informing on Jews was deemed not only acceptable but patriotic.[15] In June 1940, there were approximately 300,000 Jews living in France, somewhat more than a third of whom were not French citizens. Together they constituted less than 1 percent of the general population of forty million.

In August 1940, the Marchandeau Law, which forbade attacks in the press on religions and ethnic groups, was repealed and an anti-Semitic campaign quickly ensued. In October 1940, the Vichy government, headed by Marshal Henri-Philippe Pétain, inspired by the 1935 Nuremberg Laws, without any pressure whatsoever from the Nazis, alone among all occupied Western European nations began to pass its own anti-Semitic laws. Whereas the Nazis had defined a Jew as a person with three Jewish grandparents, the Vichy government considered a person Jewish with only two Jewish grandparents if that person had a Jewish spouse. This made it easier to be identified as a Jew in Vichy France than in the Occupied Zone,

15. In addition to Ousby, Jackson, Burrin, and Gildea on Vichy and its treatment of the Jews, I have read with profit Robert O. Paxton, *Vichy France: Old Guard and New Order, 1940–1944* (New York: Columbia University Press, 1972); Richard J. Golsan, ed., *Memory, The Holocaust, and French Justice: The Bousquet and Touvier Affairs* (Hanover, N.H.: University Press of New England, 1996); Susan Zuccotti, *The Holocaust, the French, and the Jews* (New York: Harper Collins, 1993); Richard Weisberg, *Vichy Law and the Holocaust in France* (New York: New York University Press, 1996). I have relied most heavily on Michael R. Marrus and Robert O. Paxton, *Vichy France and the Jews* (Stanford, Calif.: Stanford University Press, 1981).

where the Nazi regulation held. It also meant that in France as well as in Germany and all other occupied countries, for the first time in the modern world, Jews were defined by heredity, fixed in their Judaism, no longer free to choose to be or not to be Jews.

Having defined them in a spirit of deep-seated collaboration with the Nazis, Vichy then set out to marginalize Jews in France and to diminish their influence. All Jews, French and foreign, were banned from most middle-class professions, the military, national education, and public service. They were obliged to register and were forbidden to relocate without reporting their addresses. They were refused admission to cinemas, theaters, restaurants, and museums. Foreign Jews were interned in concentration camps throughout the country. In June 1942, in the Occupied Zone, Jews from the age of six onward were forced to wear the yellow star. This was never done in the Unoccupied Zone, however, although the identity papers of Jewish people there were marked with the word *JUIF* in red capital letters. Lest we be tempted to think that there was no collaboration with the Nazis by the French people themselves, the quotas of Jews in each profession were regulated by non-Jews in that profession, and when some 40,000 private Jewish businesses were "Aryanized" and other Jewish properties confiscated, there was no shortage of French non-Jews ready to fleece their compatriots. Although France was not a *nation* of collaborators, Robert Gildea is correct to insist that "anti-Semitism was not confined to the Vichy regime."[16] In addition to this active collaboration, during the two years in which Jews in France were stripped of their rights, their property, and their dignity, there were no organized public protests against these measures. Most people were either indifferent to the plight of the Jews or afraid to speak out. Until the major roundups and deportations began in July 1942, even the French Catholic hierarchy made no public objection to Vichy's treatment of the Jews.

16. Gildea, *Marianne in Chains*, 228.

Although several roundups had taken place and some convoys had already left France before the summer of 1942, it was the infamous Vel d'Hiv roundup of July 16–17, 1942, that finally caught the nation's attention. On these two days, roughly nine thousand French policemen arrested over thirteen thousand Jews in Paris, most of whom were held in the Vélodrome d'Hiver, an indoor sporting arena in the 15th *arrondissement;* 12,884 were eventually sent to Drancy and other camps in France and finally deported to Auschwitz. Even though French textbooks continued until 1983 to declare that Jewish deportations had been an entirely German affair,[17] in reality, they had been almost entirely a French police affair and never could have been so effective had they not been so. French police cooperated eagerly with the Nazis in rounding up and deporting Jews not only from the Occupied Zone but, alone among all occupied nations in Western Europe, from the Unoccupied Zone as well. They were responsible, just in 1942, for the deportation of 41,951 Jews from France.[18]

If any one thing in particular underscores the deep-seated anti-Semitism, cruelty, and cynicism of the Vichy regime, it is the decision made by Vichy's second-in-command, Pierre Laval. When the Germans demanded the deportation of Jewish males aged sixteen to sixty and Jewish females sixteen to fifty-five, Laval deported Jewish children along with their parents on the pretext of keeping Jewish families together. As a result, some ten thousand more Jewish children were deported than would have been had only German guidelines been followed. A total of 11,402 Jewish children (seventeen years of age and under) were ultimately deported. Only three hundred survived.[19] In addition, Laval reneged on promises he had made to differentiate between foreign Jews and French Jews when it came to deportation. Both were deported from both zones. In

17. Ian Buruma, "The Vichy Syndrome," *Tikkun* 10 (1995): 47.
18. Jackson, *France: The Dark Years,* 360.
19. Serge Klarsfeld, *French Children of the Holocaust: A Memorial* (New York: New York University Press, 1996), 8.

the end, one-third of the 76,000 Jews deported from France were French citizens. As Philippe Burrin observes: "[Laval] sacrificed the Jews to the needs of his own politics with a lack of scruples and deep indifference."[20] Laval was more of an opportunist than a rabid anti-Semite but this distinction must have been lost on those whom he deported.

Soon after the Vel d'Hiv roundup, several protests were made by a few members of the Catholic hierarchy, Cardinal Gerlier of Lyon, Monsignor Théas of Montauban, and Monsignor Saliège of Toulouse among them. There were other, nonecclesiastical protests against the brutality and physical ill-treatment of Jews now taking place in the streets. Even though a good number of French people wanted foreign Jews out of the country, many of them were outraged by the barbarity of the French police and stunned by dozens of spectacular public suicides. Shortly thereafter, however, these protests died down. Church leaders went back to their support of the head of the Vichy government, Marshal Pétain.

The nature of the Occupation changed suddenly and radically in November 1942 when, after the Allies had landed in North Africa, the Germans descended to occupy the southern part of the country as well. Although not operative until February 1943, in September 1942 the Compulsory Labor Service (Service du travail obligatoire, STO) was passed. This legislation made all French men aged eighteen to fifty and all French women twenty-one to thirty-five eligible for mobilization for work in Germany or in German factories in France. Roughly 650,000 civilian French workers were eventually sent to Germany.[21] This was the exodus from France that preoccupied the French people and perhaps more than anything definitively turned them against the occupiers. The French Catholic Church too offered more vocal protest against this practice than against the deportation of the Jews. However, even though the French Resistance

20. Burrin, France Under the Germans, 74.
21. Jackson, France: The Dark Years, 1.

never derailed or otherwise impeded a single one of the eighty-five convoys that took the 76,000 Jews from France to the death camps, there was much more sympathy for and solidarity with Jews in France from mid-1942 to mid-1944 than there had been between mid-1940 and mid-1942.

Whatever its motivations might have been, from 1940 to 1944 the Vichy government treated Jews in France, especially foreign Jews, exactly as they were treated in Germany: they were humiliated, uprooted, dispossessed of their dignity and their goods, cast into internment camps, and, finally, exiled to the gas chambers. The earliest sustained Christian voice of opposition to Vichy's anti-Semitism came at the outset in June 1940 from individual French Protestants throughout the country—members of the hierarchy, lower clergy, and laity. The villagers on the plateau Vivarais-Lignon, armed only with the strength of their beliefs, in full view of the Vichy government and, eventually, neighboring storm troopers, were among those who refused to accept the invincibility of evil and brute power. They saved the lives of about five thousand refugees, approximately 3,500 of whom were Jewish, many of them children.

In 1936, 95 percent of Le Chambon-sur-Lignon's 2,721 people were Protestant and roughly half of them were poor peasants living on farms or in small hamlets scattered over many square miles around the village. Although throughout France no more than 2 percent of the overall population was Protestant, here, on the plateau Vivarais-Lignon, 38 percent of the population (24,058) was Protestant.[22] This Protestant enclave was on a high plateau with less than forty inhabitants per square kilometer whose twelve parishes covered an extremely isolated area of small villages and remote farms.

One of the most inspiring leaders of the nonviolent rescue mission was André Trocmé, the pastor of the Reformed Church of

22. François Boulet, "Quelques éléments statistiques," in Bolle et al., *Le Plateau Vivarais-Lignon*, 287.

André and Magda Trocmé in the late 1930s in Le Chambon-sur-Lignon. *Courtesy of Nelly Trocmé Hewett.*

France in Le Chambon-sur-Lignon who, with his assistant pastor, Edouard Theis, founded a private coeducational school, the Ecole Nouvelle Cévenole, on the principles of nonviolence, conscientious objection, internationalism, fellowship, and peace. Trocmé and Theis thus became catalysts in the rescue mission in and around Le Chambon-sur-Lignon. But, once begun, that mission developed on its own, with numerous individuals working independently. Each of the twelve parishes on the plateau had its own minister and rescue operation. Gérard Bollon, a major historian of the plateau, maintains that "fifteen pastors with seven foreign pastors, principally Swiss, did the same rescue work in their parishes as Trocmé did in his."[23]

While these other ministers headed rescue missions in their villages, in the area of Le Chambon-sur-Lignon Trocmé and Theis preached resistance against the hatred and naked destruction of the Third Reich. They rallied their flock against appeasement, violence, and violation of the Gospels. As Hallie points out, the official handbook of the Hitler Youth organization states that "the foundation of the National Socialist outlook on life is the perception of the unlikeness of men" (273). Trocmé and Theis taught the absolute equality and dignity of all human beings. Their aggressive nonviolence and active pacifism helped to make the plateau the safest place in France for Jewish children, even during the last year of the Occupation when, sought by the German police, Trocmé and Theis were forced to go into hiding.

It is unfortunate that the publication of Hallie's *Lest Innocent Blood Be Shed* brought charges of "sanctification" of André Trocmé, and then his vilification. Hallie's book is not, as some have claimed, an "adaptation" of André Trocmé's unpublished "Mémoires."[24] The

23. Unpublished interview with Barbara Barnett (July 1993). A copy of this interview is in my possession.
24. Serge Bernard, "Territoire et marquage identitaire," 100. Regarding other authors critical of Hallie and Trocmé whose work has been incorporated into Bernard's writing, see Oscar Rosowsky, "Les faux papiers d'identité au Chambon-sur-Lignon

two major sources of Hallie's book are the "Mémoires" and the lengthy tapes recorded by Magda Trocmé. Hallie lists many central sources that go far beyond the Trocmé family. "Aside from these two sources," he writes, "there were many whose testimony is central to the book . . . Edouard Theis, Burns Chalmers, Richard Unsworth, Daniel Isaac, Roger Darcissac, M. and Mme Ernest Chazot, Mme Georgette Barraud, Mme Eyraud, Mme Marion, Mlle Marion, Miss Maber" (295–96). Even though Hallie focuses on Trocmé and Theis, he insists on the importance of the houses of refuge, the *pensions,* the surrounding farms where children were hidden, and all those who worked in them. Hallie mentions explicitly that "it is misleading to think about Trocmé as an isolated leader" (98) and he elucidates all the help that Trocmé received and needed: from the Quakers, the American Congregationalists, the YMCA, the Fellowship of Reconciliation, those who made false papers. At times, Trocmé could do nothing "without the presbyterial council" (167) and a parish that supported that council. Everything in Hallie's account indicates that this was a collective venture. Although Trocmé "had inspired [the rescue mission]," writes Hallie, "he had not made it what it was, the way Barot and others had made La Cimade" [a largely Protestant organization, mostly composed of women, that helped refugees in every possible way] (195). Hallie did not isolate Trocmé from all the other rescue participants, sanctify him, and narrate his legend.

The same critic charges Trocmé himself with the narration of his own legend. Trocmé's manner of narrating the 1940–44 events in his unpublished "Mémoires," it is asserted, depicts the same characteristics found in Hallie's narration (isolation and highlighting of one individual, exaggeration of that individual's contributions while obscuring the rest of the picture) and leads equally to

1942–1944," in Bolle et al., *Le Plateau Vivarais-Lignon,* 232–61; Roger Debiève, *Mémoires meurtries, mémoire trahie* (Paris: L'Harmattan, 1995), passim; Jacques Poujol, *Protestants dans la France en guerre 1939–1945,* passim.

"the construction of legendary memory." Nothing could be further from the truth, however, than the claim that reading Trocmé's "Mémoires" gives the impression that "the Trocmés were alone against everyone else; without them, the children would not have been saved."[25] Any objective reader of either André Trocmé's "Mémoires" or Magda Trocmé's "Souvenirs Autobiographiques" would be nothing less than astounded by this assertion which, curiously enough, was made before either of these volumes was available to the public.[26] As was also true in Hallie's account, both André and Magda Trocmé make frequent references to others without whom the rescue work in the area would never have been accomplished. Trocmé's construction of his own legend by recycling the image of a legendary figure from the Wars of Religion leading his people at a moment of crisis is nothing but the figment of a distorted imagination. One will not find it in Trocmé's "Mémoires."

It is time to jettison all myths, positive and negative, regarding all the people on the plateau. In the aftermath of the misrepresentations regarding André Trocmé, it is also time to give him his due. Sixty-two years after the end of the war, Trocmé is remembered as one of the principal architects of the rescue mission on the plateau. Before writing the second published version of his "André Trocmé: un violent vaincu par Dieu," which appeared in 1995, Georges Menut spoke to thirty people who knew Trocmé during the 1939–44 period and sent out a questionnaire to 130 others who knew him at that time. Seventy-five percent responded. Trocmé is characterized as "a superactive individual capable of mobilizing an entire region" who "encouraged [the other pastors] to help out the Jewish people"

25. Serge Bernard, "La Construction de la mémoire légendaire au Chambon-sur-Lignon. Mise en scène et reconstitution de l'histoire" (master's thesis, Université Paris 7, Jussieu, 2000), 93.

26. André Trocmé, "Mémoires"; Magda Trocmé Grilli di Cortona, "Souvenirs Autobiographiques." Both of these unpublished volumes are housed in the Peace Collection at the Swarthmore College Library and have been available to the public since August 2001.

and the other refugees on the plateau. "He incited them to act and to offer shelter."[27] When asked why they sheltered Jewish people in their homes, Protestants on the plateau frequently responded: "because Pastor Trocmé asked us to do so and we couldn't refuse him."[28] Menut is hardly alone in reporting the major influence of Trocmé on the rescue mission on the plateau. Olivier Hatzfeld calls Trocmé "a man of action" who, with Magda, was considered "the leader of the community." Local Resistance leader Pierre Fayol saw him in the same light.[29] Gérard Bollon credits all the ministers on the plateau for their rescue work, but singles out Trocmé as "a leader," "a visionary," "perhaps the principal organizer," "the soul of Le Chambon-sur-Lignon" with "a stature that went beyond a single parish."[30]

From the very beginning, June 23, 1940, the day after the armistice, more than two years before the official September 22, 1942, letter of protest from French Protestant leader Marc Boegner, Trocmé and Theis encouraged resistance to Vichy and spoke out publicly against Vichy's treatment of the Jews. They were influenced and inspired by Pastor Martin Niemöller and the Confessing Church, and as Christian pacifist conscientious objectors, they were dedicated to fighting the Nazis nonviolently. Trocmé, who believed that "the role of the Church was to struggle for social justice,"[31] led by example. In a letter, most probably written in February 1943, to his older brother Robert, who lived in the original Occupied Zone, but addressed, for precautionary reasons, to the fictitious Simone, Trocmé explains the rescue work going on in his home:

27. Georges Menut, "André Trocmé: un violent vaincu par Dieu," *Le Chambon-sur-Lignon: Un village pas comme les autres* (Le Chambon-sur-Lignon: Société d'Histoire de la Montagne, 1995), 67–68; 84; 69. The first version, with the same title, appeared in 1992 in *Le Plateau Vivarais-Lignon*, 378–400.

28. Georges Menut, "Accueillir ou rejeter l'étranger," in *Le Chambon-sur-Lignon: un village pas comme les autres*, 58.

29. Letter of September 13, 2003, from Olivier Hatzfeld to Patrick Cabanel.

30. Unpublished interview with Barbara Barnett (July 1993).

31. André Trocmé, "Mémoires," 269. On the influence of Niemöller, see p. 339.

You know, perhaps, that this past summer we were able to help out about sixty Jewish people who had taken refuge in our home: we hid them, provided them with fresh supplies, rescued them from deportation groups and often led them to a safe country . . . By the tens, by the hundreds, Jews are being directed toward Le Chambon. My usual ministry has ceased completely because of this situation. Normally, in the summer, my dining room has been transformed into a waiting room (10–15 people a day). Now that's the situation all year round.[32]

Trocmé's imagery here justifies Sabine Zeitoun's observation that "the presbytery became the heart of the village for the reception and then the dispersion of the refugees into the homes of the villagers and the peasants."[33] The Hôtel May and Mme Barraud's boarding house, Beau Soleil, were two other such places.

In his unpublished "Mémoires," which were mainly written twenty to twenty-five years after the events and were conceived of as a private document composed solely for his children and grandchildren, Trocmé says that one should not speak of the rescue work one has done: "Haven't others also resisted? That Salvationist, that pastor, didn't he die in a concentration camp? Are you still among the living? Then keep quiet about it."[34] When in early March 1971, Trocmé, who was living in Geneva, learned that he was to be recognized by Yad Vashem as a "Righteous Gentile," he wrote to the Jewish historian Anny Latour:

Why me and not the host of humble peasants of the Haute-Loire region, who did as much and more than I did? Why not my wife whose behavior was much more heroic than mine? Why not my colleague Edouard Theis with whom I shared all responsibilities?

32. Magda Trocmé, "Souvenirs Autobiographiques," 247. Although it appears in Magda's text, the letter was written by André Trocmé.
33. Sabine Zeitoun, *Ces enfants qu'il fallait sauver* (Paris: Albin Michel, 1989), 218.
34. André Trocmé, "Mémoires," 530.

I can only accept the Righteous Gentile medal in the name of all those who stuck their necks out and risked death for our unjustly persecuted brothers and sisters. Despite everything, I still feel guilty for what was not done for them.

Trocmé then asks Mme Latour to intervene so that the ceremony, originally planned for the Israeli embassy in Bern, can take place in Le Chambon-sur-Lignon. Later in the month, when he learns that the ceremony will take place in Le Chambon-sur-Lignon, Trocmé writes to the Israeli General Consul in Paris: "The ceremony should be held at the town hall so as to bring together all those who helped shelter and save Jewish refugees during the war. The inhabitants of the neighboring villages: Le Mazet, Tence, Mars, Saint-Agrève, Devesset should also be invited." These letters alone refute the ill-founded charges regarding the so-called propensity in André Trocmé to exaggerate the role he played in the rescue mission on the plateau.[35]

Georges Menut's advice regarding Trocmé is sagacious: "Let's remember him without making him either a god or a monument."[36] While Trocmé and Theis were extremely influential, very little if anything could have been accomplished without the people on the plateau. The congregation in Le Chambon-sur-Lignon, for example, was indeed up to the task. The scattered groups formerly created for Bible study in the distant areas of the parish became one of the important communication networks for locating hiding places and guiding the terrified foreigners to safety. Not everyone in Le Chambon hid refugees, but a great majority of the village was actively involved in the rescue mission, including, among others, teachers who enrolled foreign students with obviously false papers in their classes, town hall employees who issued additional food tickets to fami-

35. Letter from André Trocmé to Mme A. Latour (March 8, 1971); undated letter from André Trocmé to the Israeli General Consul in Paris. Copies of both of these letters are in my possession.
36. Georges Menut, "André Trocmé: un violent vaincu par Dieu," 95.

lies who were hiding Jews, and storekeepers who "forgot" to ask for rationing tickets. In fact, after the summer of 1942, sheltering Jews on the plateau was the norm, not the exception. Once the rescue operation began, it seemed to spread indiscriminately everywhere on the plateau. There was a constant flow of refugees, some staying only a few days, others for months or for years. The countryside somehow absorbed thousands of refugees over the war years.

The pastors, with help from national and international organizations, established houses of refuge to feed, clothe, protect, and educate young children who had been removed from internment camps in southern France, sometimes just before their parents were deported. By the middle of the Occupation, there were seven such houses near or in Le Chambon. They were financed by Quakers, American Congregationalists, the Swiss Red Cross, and even national governments like Sweden. In addition, there were more than a dozen *pensions,* or boarding houses, toward the center of the village that housed children and adolescent refugees of both sexes. Finally, in addition to the many private homes that sheltered Jews, some keeping children for years, there was the Ecole Nouvelle Cévenole, where a fair portion of the student population on scholarship was Jewish and whose enrollment grew annually, from 18 in 1938 to 350 in 1944.[37] Whereas others have spoken perceptively of the "banality of evil" during the Holocaust, we can speak of the "ordinariness of goodness" on the plateau. Based on simple notions of common decency—strangers who came to the door were housed and fed—goodness spread from farm to farm, from person to person, from one act to the next.[38]

In addition to sheltering Jews, the people on the plateau also

37. See François Boulet, "Quelques éléments statistiques," in Bolle et al., *Le Plateau Vivarais-Lignon,* 288.

38. Along these lines, see François Rochat and André Modigliani, "The Ordinary Quality of Resistance: From Milgram's Laboratory to the Village of Le Chambon," *Journal of Social Issues* 51 (1995): 195–212, and David R. Blumenthal, *The Banality of Good and Evil: Moral Lessons from the Shoah and Jewish Tradition* (Washington, D.C.: Georgetown University Press, 1999).

hid Communists, anti-Fascist Germans, Spanish republicans, other stateless people, and, as of February 1943, Service du travail obligatoire (STO) defaulters. They also practiced noncooperation with the Vichy government. In Le Chambon, the ministers disobeyed orders to ring the church bell in honor of the chief of state. At the Ecole Nouvelle Cévenole, they refused to put a picture of Pétain on the wall and would not enforce the mandatory saluting of the flag. In August 1942, three weeks after the Vel d'Hiv roundup, a group of students from the school protested the shocking treatment of Parisian Jews in a letter, at least inspired if not written by André Trocmé, that they presented to the visiting Vichy Minister of Youth, Georges Lamirand. The letter informed him that there were Jews among them but that the villagers did not differentiate between Jews and non-Jews and in any event would never turn them in if asked to do so because that would violate Gospel teachings. Lamirand claimed this was not his affair and that they would have to speak to Prefect Bach, who promptly threatened to have Trocmé arrested if he were to disobey orders. Two weeks later, Trocmé was summoned to the town hall, where he was once again menaced with arrest, this time by the Vichy police chief, if he failed to turn over Jews hiding in the village.[39]

Trocmé was finally arrested, with Theis and Roger Darcissac, the director of the public school in Le Chambon-sur-Lignon, in the early evening of February 13, 1943. They spent almost five weeks in the internment camp Saint-Paul d'Eyjeaux, near Limoges, a political reeducation camp, not a forced labor camp, where 75 percent of the inmates were Communists. They were released unexpectedly on March 16 after a telegram arrived from Vichy, just before the camp was liquidated and the prisoners deported.[40] Later, both Trocmé and Theis spent ten months in hiding. It was not, however, "the fear of being harassed" that sent André Trocmé into hiding in Au-

39. André Trocmé, "Mémoires," 361–66.
40. Ibid., 231–33.

gust 1943.[41] It was rather that "the Reformed Church (in the person of Maurice Rohr) asked them [Trocmé and Theis] to leave the village."[42] When one realizes how precarious life was for these village leaders and that Jews and non-Jews living in Le Chambon-sur-Lignon were deported and gassed in the death camps, one wonders how anyone can possibly maintain that "the risks incurred only became apparent after the war."[43]

While there were openly collective actions undertaken on the plateau, much that happened there was done under a cloak of secrecy. People in the area often did not know about the rescue efforts of their neighbors. They suspected that others must have agreed to shelter the latest arrivals but did not know who or where. They did not talk about it much either during the war, when they used passwords and codes to do so,[44] or after the war. Furthermore, no permanent records were kept. Although many people never procured them, there were several suppliers of false identity papers on the plateau. Oscar Rosowsky, a teenager in hiding under the name of Jean-Claude Plunne, was the main provider of false papers but several others, including Roger Darcissac, also fabricated them. The rescue mission involved a mixture of candor and evasiveness. The people on the plateau did not conceal the fact that they sheltered Jews, but when the Vichy police came looking for them, the refugees had disappeared into their hiding places. The reticent nature of these isolated mountain people was a definite asset in a system where privacy and unspoken consensus, candor and concealment, were necessary. It worked well in the village known to the Germans

41. Serge Bernard, *La Construction de la mémoire légendaire,* 20.

42. E-mail to author from Annik Flaud, November 15, 2003, citing a letter from Edouard Theis's daughter, Jeanne, to Nevin Sayre. See too André Trocmé, "Mémoires," 402.

43. Jean-Pierre Houssel, "La résistance civile sur le Plateau: paysans et patriotes," in Cabanel and Gervereau, *La Deuxième Guerre mondiale,* 114.

44. See Daniel Curtet, "Témoignage d'un ancien Pasteur," in Bolle et al., *Le Plateau Vivarais-Lignon,* 54–67.

and the Vichy officials, Philip Hallie points out, as "that nest of Jews in Protestant country" (1994; p. 10). In this ecumenical village, no villager ever denounced a single refugee or a person concealing refugees.

It is important to know something about Protestantism and its history in Catholic France to understand not only why the Huguenots, in particular, identified with the persecuted Jews, but also why they were so successful in sheltering them. Protestants were persecuted in France from the 1530s until 1598, when Henri IV signed the Edict of Nantes, giving them the right to practice their religion openly. Louis XIV revoked that edict in 1685 and Protestants were again persecuted until the revolution in 1789. In 1560, there were sixteen million French people, one million of whom were Protestant. In 1940, there were forty million French people but at most only eight hundred thousand Protestants. During the times of persecution, there were huge emigrations into Holland, Germany, northern Italy, England, Canada, and the United States. Following the revocation of the Edict of Nantes, for example, roughly 200,000 Huguenots left the country.[45] Those who could not afford to flee to foreign countries and who hid in the most inhospitable areas of the country survived on cunning, secrecy, and silence. Living clandestinely, they cultivated a strong distrust of governments.

As daily readers of the Bible, French Protestants knew the Hebrew Bible well and were therefore familiar with Jewish history. A persecuted minority throughout the greater portion of their own history, they felt close to marginalized peoples, and many of them particularly identified with the Jews, whom they recognized as the chosen people of God. Patrick Cabanel notes magnificently regard-

45. On the history of Protestant emigration from France in times of persecution, see *La Diaspora des Huguenots: les réfugiés protestants de France et leur dispersion dans le monde (16e–18e siècles)*, ed. Eckart Birnstiel and Chrystel Bernat (Paris: Champion, 2001). See too *Memory and Identity: The Huguenots in France and the Atlantic Diaspora*, ed. Bertrand Van Ruymbeke and Randy J. Sparks (Columbia: University of South Carolina Press, 2003).

ing the plateau Vivarais-Lignon: "The Hebrews had been there for four centuries, when the Jews arrived."[46] If the Hebrew Bible is such a source of inspiration for the Protestants of France, why did it not rouse the Protestants in Germany against Hitler? For one reason, the Protestants of Germany had never been collectively persecuted as had been French Protestants, nor were they a minority. Then, as Patrick Cabanel points out, there is a radical difference between Luther's view of the Jews and that of Calvin. Whereas Luther's anti-Judaism was notorious, "Calvin insists on continuity between the two testaments and envisages that God's plan for humanity, distinguishing between the elect and the damned, held for the salvation of the Jews as well as that of Christians." For Cabanel, then, Calvin was the first "to call into question the teaching of scorn" for the Jews that continued in other Christian faiths into the twentieth century.[47] French Protestants refer to the 1685–1789 period of their history as "the desert," which is a clear indication of their identification and solidarity with the Jews. When the Jewish refugees were taken on the three-hundred-kilometer journey from Le Chambon-sur-Lignon to Switzerland, as Pierre Sauvage portrays beautifully in *Weapons of the Spirit*, they were following the same route taken by refugee Protestants hundreds of years earlier.

Roughly one-third of the Protestants in the area of Le Chambon-sur-Lignon were not Huguenots but Darbyites, evangelical followers of the nineteenth-century English preacher John Darby. They were radical fundamentalists who did not believe in the clergy and were obviously not parishioners of Trocmé and Theis. They held their own religious meetings and simply read the Scriptures and tried to live by them. Given the solidarity between the two persecuted minorities, the French Huguenots and the Jewish people, it is striking that the Darbyites responded more promptly to Trocmé's call to shelter

46. Patrick Cabanel, "L'Israël des Cévennes, réflexions sur une «exception huguenote» face aux juifs," in Cabanel and Gervereau, *La Deuxième Guerre mondiale*, 212.
47. Ibid., 217–18.

the Jews than did the members of his own church. Also odd, for the same reason, is *not* the September 1942 public condemnation, by National Protestant Federation President Marc Boegner, of Vichy's anti-Semitism and outrageous treatment of Jews, but rather its date. Why did this public objection not take place two years earlier?[48]

Be that as it may, there was a long tradition of sheltering the persecuted on the plateau Vivarais-Lignon. Not only had the plateau served as a place of refuge for victimized Huguenots throughout the centuries of their persecution in Catholic France but it had sheltered Catholic priests during the period of the French Revolution and had also taken in, among others, Alsatian refugees in 1914 and refugees from Spain beginning in 1936.[49] This proud tradition of sanctuary extended to children. From the end of the nineteenth century onward, thanks in large measure to Pastor Louis Comte, undernourished and underprivileged children, mostly from the poor mining area of Saint Etienne, came to the plateau for health reasons. A former history and geography teacher at the Ecole Nouvelle Cévenole, Bernard Galland, also explains that before there were summer camps in the area, many undernourished children (3,734 in 1935 alone, Bollon notes) came to live on farms to play, guard sheep, run errands, and build up their health.[50] As a result, by the late 1930s, many boarding houses for children and vacation camps had long been established in the area. The plateau was then, in a sense, ready to receive the Jewish children when they arrived. But

48. See, for example, Hallie, *Lest Innocent Blood Be Shed*, 95–98; 182–83, and Daniel Besson, "Les Assemblées des Frères, darbystes et ravinistes, et l'accueil des Juifs," in Bolle et al., *Le Plateau Vivarais-Lignon*, 86–89.

Le Chambon-sur-Lignon researcher and archivist Annik Flaud does not believe that Boegner, who preferred to work diplomatically behind the scenes, ever "protested publicly in the name of the French Protestant Church." Flaud refers to Boegner's 1941 letter to the Grand Rabbi and Admiral Darlan and his two 1942 letters to Pétain. I am referring to his second 1942 letter to Pétain, which was read in the pulpit.

49. Gérard Bollon, "La tradition d'accueil avant la guerre," in Bolle et al., *Le Plateau Vivarais-Lignon*, 151–60.

50. Ibid., 154. For Bernard Galland, I refer to his unpublished interview with Barbara Barnett (July 1993), a copy of which is in my possession.

everything regarding their arrival, lodging, and the nature of their residency would be quite different.

There has been much debate as to when the refugees arrived on the plateau. Despite the rather common belief, even among scholars,[51] that the Jewish refugees came after the Vel d'Hiv roundup in July 1942, in reality they came much earlier. Although it is true that there was more sympathy for the plight of Jews in France after July 1942 and evidence of much more rescue activity after that date in Le Chambon-sur-Lignon and more generally throughout the country, spiritual resistance to the Nazis began much earlier on the plateau and lasted through the entire length of time Hitler was in power. According to Annik Flaud, for example, "there were three or four German political refugees in Mme Barraud's boarding house in 1934."[52] The enrollment records at the Ecole Nouvelle Cévenole show an amazing increase in student numbers: 18 in 1938, 40 in 1939, 150 in 1940, and 250 in 1941.[53] Many of these students were Jewish refugees in hiding. In the winter of 1940–41, several pastors began relations with organizations such as La Cimade and the Quakers that were already working in the internment camps in the south of France and would eventually bring refugees to the plateau. In May 1941, for example, the house called La Guespy opened its doors to welcome eighteen children from these camps.[54] All the evidence indicates that there were Jews hiding on the plateau in the late 1930s, many more in 1941 and the first half of 1942, and much greater numbers after July 1942, as the February 1943 letter written by André Trocmé to his brother Robert indicates.

The saddest part of the revisionist reading of what happened on the plateau is its utter inability to fathom the spiritual dimension

51. Jean-Pierre Houssel, "La résistance civile sur le Plateau: paysans et patriotes," 113.

52. E-mail to author from Annik Flaud, October 9, 2003.

53. François Boulet, "Quelques elements statistiques," in Bolle et al., *Le Plateau Vivarais-Lignon*, 288.

54. E-mail to author from Annik Flaud, September 2, 2003.

of this activity. From the very outset of his thesis, Serge Bernard explains this phenomenon in materialistic terms: expressions such as "common currency" *(monnaie courante),* "commercial contingencies" *(contingences commerciales),* and "tourist economy" *(économie d'accueil)*[55] signal throughout his work the fundamental monetization of the phenomenon of rescue on the plateau Vivarais-Lignon.

There is no question that Le Chambon-sur-Lignon enjoyed dynamic tourism long before, during, and after World War II. During the war, there were many tourists in and around the area. Hotels and restaurants did well. Tourists and, in a very small number of cases, refugees brought large sums of money to the area, thus making the local economy a relatively flourishing one. Bernard cites texts written by André Trocmé and Pierre Fayol to demonstrate that, comparatively speaking, prices were extremely high in Le Chambon-sur-Lignon but food was more readily available there than in the cities.[56] Since there were many nonresidents in the area, it was easier for refugees to hide. More generally, the area offered refugees, most of whom worked in some capacity on the plateau, hospitality, food, a vacation atmosphere, and a safe place, with a nearby forest, where it was much easier to avoid roundups than in large cities.

Bernard focuses on the tourist economy and maintains that, by a process of "sublimation" (or moral elevation), what is a materialist phenomenon ("tourist economy"/*économie d'accueil*) has been represented as a spiritual reality, a "reception tradition" *(tradition d'accueil)* for minorities and persecuted persons.[57] For Bernard, this passage from tourism, the indispensable economic resource of the area, to "Protestant hagiography," not only deforms the past but also serves to create a more flourishing "tourist economy" in the present. In the final analysis, Bernard mistakes "means" for "ends."

55. Serge Bernard, *La Construction de la mémoire légendaire,* 4; 6; 113.
56. Ibid., 47–51.
57. Ibid., 107.

Food and the ability to offer shelter were necessary material means to accomplish a specific end, the rescue of thousands of refugees. If there had not been sufficient food, possibilities for shelter, and a nearby forest, it would not have been possible to rescue so many refugees. The spiritual nature, the moral courage, and the elevated concept of human solidarity of the inhabitants, however, accounted for what happened here from 1939 to 1944. The refugees could not have been sheltered without these material means but they were not sheltered because of them. Once again, failing to distinguish between "tourist reception" *(accueil estival)* and what I would call "shelter and rescuing hospitality" *(accueil sauvetage),* Bernard remains fixated on what was necessary to the doing of what was being done but subordinate to the higher purpose for which the thing was done.

The people on the plateau did what they did because these particular Christians believed that to do otherwise would be to act against their religious conscience. In the winter of 1940–41, André Trocmé went to the offices of the American Friends Service Committee in Marseille because he wanted to work with them to bring desperately needed supplies and consolation to Jews being held in internment camps in southern France. As soon as the Germans took over in June 1940, foreign Jews were rounded up and interned in concentration camps throughout the country. By the end of 1940, there were roughly 30,000 foreign Jews in these camps, three thousand of whom would die there. The conditions in these camps, entirely run by French personnel, were deplorable. Christian groups, such as La Cimade, the YMCA, the Quakers, and the Jewish group Oeuvre de secours aux enfants (OSE), rushed to the camps to provide food, clothing, medical care, libraries, and cultural services. Perhaps no one did more to alleviate suffering there than Madeleine Barot, the head of La Cimade, which she founded in 1939. This Protestant organization worked in the camps from August 1940 until the end of the war and played a large role in the evacuation of children from the camps, the placing of these children in homes throughout the south of France, and in many cases the smuggling of children into Switzerland.

Gurs was one of the first and largest of the internment camps established in the south of France. Situated on a high plain at the foot of the lower Pyrenees ten miles from the town of Oloron-Sainte-Marie, it was constructed to impound Spanish republicans who crossed the mountains into France after Franco's victory. When foreign Jews were rounded up and held there during the summer of 1940, the various charitable groups came to Gurs in an attempt to improve the situation. The Quakers brought large quantities of food. La Cimade established a five-thousand-volume library and brought musical instruments for recitals. OSE offered much need-ed psychological counseling to all internees, especially children.[58] But the conditions remained horrible. Survivors speak of constant hunger, head lice, rats, mud, jaundice, dysentery, infectious hepati-tis, and typhus. Approximately 1,100 foreign Jews died in Gurs be-tween 1940 and 1944.

André Trocmé's trip to the Quakers in Marseille began his rela-tionship with a leading Quaker named Burns Chalmers, who told him at a subsequent meeting in Nîmes: "We can get people out of the camps but nobody wants them. It is dangerous to take them. Is your village prepared to do such a thing? Do you wish to be that community?" Trocmé assured him that Le Chambon would be will-ing to serve in that capacity. Chalmers told him to find houses of refuge and the people to run them and the Quakers and the Fellow-ship of Reconciliation would support them financially. Trocmé re-turned home, where the elders of the church voted immediately to

58. Jeanne Merle d'Aubigné, "Souvenirs de quelques camps en France, 1940–1947," *Quelques Actions des Protestants de France en faveur des Juifs persécutés sous l'Occupation Allemande 1940–1944* (Paris: La Cimade), ed. Violette Mouchon, 33; 40–41. Typescript in my possession.

commit the parish to this action. Le Chambon-sur-Lignon was designated as a place of refuge primarily for children. Even after America's entrance into the war, funds used to run the houses and to establish scholarships for refugee students continued to arrive from Geneva, from the Quakers, the Fellowship of Reconciliation, and the Congregationalists.[59] In his September 13, 2003, letter to Patrick Cabanel, Olivier Hatzfeld insists on the central role played by Trocmé "in the decision made by La Cimade and other organizations to entrust the children from the camps to Le Chambon-sur-Lignon"[60] and Gérard Bollon remarks that, when Trocmé returned from his meeting with Burns Chalmers in Marseille, he told his parishioners: "You must accommodate; you must protect; you must save these refugees."[61] In large measure, things happened the way they did in Le Chambon-sur-Lignon because of Trocmé and Theis, but elsewhere on the plateau others were harboring refugees on their own. Since the plateau Vivarais-Lignon had been a place of sanctuary for hundreds of years, it was only normal that, once again, the deeply held inner values of the inhabitants would result in the offering of shelter and passage to persecuted refugees.

The idea of a city of refuge originates in the Hebrew Bible and is described in some detail in Joshua 20:1–9, Numbers 35:9–31, and Deuteronomy 19:1–13, where the Jewish people were commanded to set up cities of refuge to which anyone who killed a person unintentionally could flee so as not to die by the hand of a blood avenger until there was a trial before the congregation. Perhaps because the situation in Le Chambon was different—a city of refuge was set up there for those being persecuted for no other crime than that of being Jewish—the pastors and their followers took most seriously the command of Deuteronomy 19:10: "I command you [to protect

59. André Trocmé, "Mémoires," 351–53. Magda Trocmé, "Le Chambon," in *The Courage to Care*, ed. Carol Rittner and Sondra Myers (New York: New York University Press, 1986), 103. Philip Hallie, *Lest Innocent Blood Be Shed*, 129–38.

60. Letter of September 13, 2003, from Olivier Hatzfeld to Patrick Cabanel.

61. Unpublished interview with Barbara Barnett (July 1993).

the refugee] lest innocent blood be shed in [your] land . . . thereby bringing the guilt of bloodshed upon you." Once Le Chambon became "a city of refuge," for Trocmé, Theis, and the villagers, it was not enough simply not to do evil, it was also necessary to keep others from doing harm to those who came within the city gates.

The ministers and their followers accepted the negative commandments of Exodus 20 that require us to avoid doing harm (thou shalt not kill, steal, commit adultery, etc.). Most people feel that, most of the time, this ethic of the nondoing of evil is all that is required of them. The people of Le Chambon, however, heard other voices in the Hebrew Bible, that of First Isaiah for example, urging them in addition to perform positive actions. Responding affirmatively to Cain's question—"Am I my brother's keeper?" (Genesis 4:9)—First Isaiah tells Jewish people who their brothers and sisters are: "seek justice / rescue the oppressed / defend the orphan / plead for the widow" (Isaiah 1:17), while Second Isaiah urges them "to share [their] bread with the hungry [and] bring the homeless poor into [their] house" (Isaiah 58:7). The Protestant population understood these commands, and it became known that refugees could find shelter on the plateau.[62]

The people of the area found no difference between the practical ethic emanating from the Hebrew Bible and that of the Gospels. When asked, after the war, why they did what they did, many would invariably refer to the gospel of Luke (10:25–37), where Christ cites the two great commandments in the Torah which require obedience in order to gain eternal life, the second being to love one's neighbor as oneself. Christ is then asked "Who is my neighbor?" and he responds with the parable of the Good Samaritan, in which the Jew "who has fallen into the hands of robbers" is helped by the Samaritan, a foreigner not expected to show sympathy to Jews. The sub-

---

62. Some pastors made precise reference to these passages in Isaiah. See in particular André Bettex, "Témoignage d'un ancien Pasteur," in Bolle et al., *Le Plateau Vivarais-Lignon*, 68. See in the same volume 12 and 434.

stance of these references to the gospel of Luke constitute a leitmo-tif in Pierre Sauvage's masterful *Weapons of the Spirit*. Mme Brottes and Edouard Theis cite these gospel passages explicitly in their in-terviews. The universal maxim "Love One Another," inscribed on the pediment of the front wall of the Protestant church in Le Cham-bon, had long been the guiding principle of the people in the area.

Theologically, then, the people of the plateau believed that faith without works is dead. They felt compelled to act for others, to di-minish suffering, and to put into action the principles in which they believed. Although a good number of villagers were in fact part of the violent resistance, Trocmé and Theis conscientiously objected to all violence, and told their flock from the pulpit in the famous ser-mon preached the day after the armistice: "The duty of Christians is to use the weapons of the Spirit to resist the violence that will be brought to bear on their consciences. We will resist whenever our adversaries will demand of us obedience contrary to the orders of the Gospel. We will do so without fear, but also without pride and without hate."[63] As Christian pacifists, they justified no violence whatsoever, not even the violence needed to defeat Hitler. Killing Germans, for whatever reason, was absolutely incompatible with being a Christian. Explaining what his purpose was in writing his "Mémoires," Trocmé notes: "I'm not a novelist but I'm 'charged with a mission.' My goal is not to do the work of a historian but to dem-onstrate that one can go through a war practicing nonviolence."[64]

To suggest that Trocmé's pacifism came from the United States (from peace organizations such as the American Friends Service Committee and the Fellowship of Reconciliation) is to ignore the long historical tradition of nonviolence on the plateau.[65] There had

63. Edouard Theis and André Trocmé, "Message des deux pasteurs du Chambon à leur paroisse," in Bolle et al., *Le Plateau Vivarais-Lignon,* 599. These words of Trocmé and Theis are known primarily today because they are highlighted in Pierre Sauvage's *Weapons of the Spirit.*

64. André Trocmé, "Mémoires," 371.

65. Serge Bernard, "Territoire et marquage identitaire," 99–100; 101.

to have been sympathy for nonviolence on the plateau in 1934 for André Trocmé to be accepted as pastor when it was known that he was a pacifist. He had been rejected elsewhere for that very reason. René Rémond stresses the current of pacifism among French Protestants at the time of World War II: "There was nothing in French Catholicism in 1940 that resembled the level of Protestant opinion favorable to conscientious objection and opposed to violence. There was a Protestant pacifism which had confidence in non-violence and outlawed recourse to violent actions."[66] Annik Flaud points out that this homegrown French Protestant pacifism had been embedded on the plateau Vivarais-Lignon for quite some time. "If one simply leafs through the archives of the local Société d'Histoire de la Montagne," she writes, "one discovers":

—that the War of the Camisards stopped at the zone of influence of the Consistoire de la Montagne which experienced dragonnades and persecutions but never took up arms (it was also forbidden to the participants in the assemblies of the Assemblées du Désert to be armed);

—that in April 1934 (therefore before André Trocmé's arrival) the presbyterial council officially asked the regional synod and the national synod to reconsider the Church's position on conscientious objection;

—that at the same time period, an association was created in Le Chambon-sur-Lignon under the aegis of, notably, Mr. DeFélice and Mr. Monbrison, whose aim was to come to the aid of the families of incarcerated conscientious objectors.[67]

Trocmé and Theis did what they did because they believed that hatred of other human beings brings only destruction. They hated war as a means of resolving conflict. They did not hate the so-called

66. Ibid., 103.
67. E-mails from Annik Flaud to author, September 8, 2003; November 20, 2003; November 24, 2003.

enemy. They were trying to prevent the Germans from doing more evil and were always ready to forgive them. In the last weeks of the war, when Frenchmen were finally getting revenge and Germans were being assassinated everywhere, still teaching the absolute uselessness of all hatred and the need for forgiveness, accompanied by August Bohny, Trocmé preached in German on Sundays in the nearby German prisoner of war camp, repeating the same sermon he had given that morning in French in his own church, offering the opportunity to repent, hoping to end all cycles of vengeance.

The people on the plateau, Christians, Jews, and unbelievers alike, did what they did because they believed in the dignity of all human life and the integrity of every individual. Despite their differences, they shared this vision. Never did the Protestants among them try to use their position to coerce refugee children to embrace their religion. As a survivor named Rudy Appel attests: "With the help of Pastor Trocmé, we held our own religious services on Jewish Holy Days, either in the Protestant temple or in the school."[68] This is brought out with powerful imagery in Pierre Sauvage's *Weapons of the Spirit*. Other survivors note that Jewish children were encouraged to have their own services and that sometimes Protestant services would consist only of readings from the Hebrew Bible so the Jewish children could take part without betraying their faith. These people were fully cognizant of and perfectly comfortable with the Jewish origins of their faith. Being a Christian here had nothing to do with not being Jewish and whether or not Jews accepted the Gospels—they were still considered the chosen people of God. The only real distinction that mattered on the plateau was between those who believed and those who did not believe that people "who had fallen into the hands of robbers" were as precious as themselves.

68. Carol Rittner and Sondra Myers, eds., *The Courage to Care*, 119. On this same issue, see Olivier Hatzfeld, "L'Ecole Nouvelle Cévenole: nouvelle approche," and François Boulet, "L'attitude spirituelle des protestants devant les Juifs réfugiés," in Bolle et al., *Le Plateau Vivarais-Lignon*, 164 and 407.

Although the fundamental basis for this ethical community was largely biblical, there was an enormous amount of diversity among its members, many of whom, integral agents of the rescue operation, when asked after the war why they did what they did, responded outside of any religious context.[69] There was also, in the very household of the presbytery, an interesting dichotomy between the pastor and his wife, neither of whom was native to the plateau but each of whom was an equally important catalyst in the rescue mission. André, whose mother was German, was raised in a strict Calvinist home in northern France, while Magda Trocmé Grilli di Cortona, whom André referred to as "my primitive, authentic, and creative Florentine"[70] and whose grandmother was Russian, was raised in a Catholic convent in Italy from the age of ten to eighteen.

Although she ultimately renounced Catholicism, Magda never really embraced Protestantism: "I am not a Protestant," she told André (who claimed that she remained "on the edge of faith"), "I have never been able to declare that I believe a thing of which I am not sure. I prefer not to define what I believe."[71] In fact, Magda was never deeply religious. Unlike her husband, she rarely spoke of God or even of love. "But I never close my door," she told Hallie, "never refuse to help somebody who comes to me and asks for something. This, I think, is my kind of religion." Georges Menut also viewed her in nonreligious terms: "She was above all 100 percent humanist, not in the least mystical, fleeing abstract theories ('I have other things to do'), with a very well-developed practical sense and unlimited energy."[72] For his part, Philip Hallie concluded that "despite her secularism, Magda was an effective gatekeeper for a city of refuge"

69. For an analysis of the Catholic participation in the rescue mission, see Henri Dubois, "Les communautés catholiques du Plateau," and François Boulet, "L'attitude spirituelle des protestants devant les Juifs réfugiés," in Bolle et al., *Le Plateau Vivarais-Lignon*, 82–85 and 412–13 respectively.

70. André Trocmé, "Mémoires," 50.

71. Ibid., 236.

72. Georges Menut, "André Trocmé: un violent vaincu par Dieu," 74.

(153). In her "Souvenirs Autobiographiques," Magda asserts that, in her life as the wife of a Protestant pastor, she collaborated with her husband "above all on social matters." Yet, on the same page, she insists that "my children were wrong to think that I was an unbeliever." Magda then offers a simple statement of her beliefs: "If there weren't somewhere a source of hope, justice, truth, and love, we would not have rooted in us the hope of justice, truth, and love that we find in every religion and every degree of civilization. It's that source that I call God."[73] Unlike his wife's essentially "horizontal" ethic of humanitarian conviction, André Trocmé's was a "vertical" ethic emanating directly from God's commands. Yet Trocmé had no doctrine of hell and was uncertain about the existence of an afterlife. As Hallie relates, Trocmé told the inmates of the internment camp where he was held after his arrest in February 1943: "Faith works on earth; I do not know about Heaven" (37).

A "common union" brought together on this plateau a variety of people who differed politically and religiously to achieve a mutual end. It was a group of people who embodied the ethic of Scripture, whether they were believers or not. In all that they did, Trocmé, Theis, and the firmly resolved and independent-minded mountain people demonstrated that, for them, the kingdom of God means the complete and definitive elimination of every form of vengeance and reprisal in relations between human beings on earth.

Despite the extraordinary and deep-seated collaboration between the Vichy regime and the Nazis, France had the third lowest percentage of Jews deported to the death camps. Denmark is the occupied country with the largest surviving Jewish population, 93 percent, followed by Italy, 84 percent, and then France with 76 percent of its Jewish population saved from deportation. This should be compared with Holland, Hungary, and Belgium which, respectively, lost 78 percent, 50 percent, and 45 percent of their Jewish

73. Magda Trocmé, "Souvenirs Autobiographiques," 56 and 56–57.

population.[74] Geography played a role here. France was contiguous to two countries, Switzerland and Spain, that were not persecuting Jews and some 44,000 Jews escaped from France across these two borders between 1940 and 1944.[75] In addition, when, in November 1942, the Germans occupied both zones of France, they left eight departments in the hands of the Italians who, even against the protests of the Germans themselves and the Vichy government, refused to hand over any Jews for deportation. It has been estimated that as many as thirty thousand Jews saved their lives by fleeing to these departments, which offered them safe haven until September 1943.[76]

Here again, as on the plateau Vivarais-Lignon, we must be careful to distinguish between how a thing is done and why it is accomplished. The Jews in these eight departments were not saved because the Italians were there but because the Italians refused to turn them over either to the French police or the Germans. The refugees who escaped from France into Switzerland and Spain could not have done so without the contiguous mountains, but they were able to do so only because they were aided all along the way by persons and groups, such as La Cimade, who were willing to risk their lives to save them. In each case, an unwavering belief in human solidarity and steadfast moral courage were the reasons these lives were saved in a country whose government was at best indifferent to their fate.

As of January 1, 2007, Yad Vashem had named 21,758 Gentiles "Righteous Among the Nations," singling them out as persons who risked their lives to save Jewish people during the Holocaust. After Poland (6,004) and the Netherlands (4,767), France has the largest number (2,740) of such individuals. "These figures," the Yad Vashem Web site (www.Yadvashem.org.il) states, "are not necessarily an in-

74. Jackson, *France: The Dark Years,* 362–63.
75. Robert Belot, *Aux frontières de la liberté* (Paris: Fayard, 1998), 702, n. 22.
76. On the question of Jews in Italian-run departments, see Susan Zuccotti, *The Holocaust, The French, and the Jews,* 166–68; 175–85.

dication of the actual number of Jews saved in each country, but reflect material on rescue operations made available to Yad Vashem." Everyone recognizes that the numbers represent only a fraction of the total number of persons who, in fact, risked their lives to save Jews at that moment in history. The number of rescuers may also reflect, at least in some cases, the numbers of Jews living in the particular country and the relative danger facing Jews in that country. In any event, it must never be forgotten that in France, the occupied country where the collaboration with the Nazis was the greatest, thousands of French people did risk their lives to save Jews.

In his "Mémoires," André Trocmé points out that immediately after the war: "Everyone discovered that they possessed the soul of a resister; the *maquis* [underground] was glorified; de Gaulle praised to the heavens . . . everyone believed that they had driven out the Nazis." While the Gaullists and Communists argued about which one had done the most to liberate France, few were interested in hearing about nonviolent resistance against the Nazis and Vichy, what Trocmé refers to as "conscientious objection identical to that of those who preferred prison to murder, but applied to other objects: conscientious objection to injustice, to lies, to political and racial persecutions."[77] More than sixty years later, it is certainly time to acknowledge that not all French World War II heroes were in the Resistance. Thousands of them also risked their lives rescuing potential victims of the Nazis and the Vichy government.

Pierre Fayol, one of the leaders of the armed Resistance in Le Chambon-sur-Lignon and a Jewish refugee himself, refers to these other heroes as "the unknown Resisters" and asks that they too be collectively recognized throughout the country as members of the armed Resistance have already been. "French cities have been decorated with the French Resistance Medal in recognition of the collective actions of their inhabitants."[78] "For 150 years," writes Ju-

77. André Trocmé, "Mémoires," 530.
78. Pierre Fayol, *Les Deux France 1936–1945* (Paris: L'Harmattan, 1994), 23; 307.

lian Jackson, "the Jews of France had looked to the state to protect them, if necessary, from the sudden anti-Semitic outbursts of civil society; in the Occupation, it was civil society that helped to protect the Jews from the State."[79] It is now time for France to recognize all those who did so.[80]

79. Jackson, *France: The Dark Years*, 380.
80. On the "Righteous Among the Nations" in France, see Lucien Lazare, *Le Livre des Justes* (Paris: Editions Jean-Claude Lattès, 1993); *Dictionnaire des Justes de France*, ed. Lucien Lazare (Paris: Fayard, 2003).

2 ⟍⟍⟍⟍

Daniel's Choice

For me, Le Chambon represents . . . a kind of contribution to the recon-
struction of our world . . . I have chosen this adventure, not because it's
an adventure, but so that I would not be ashamed of myself.

Daniel Trocmé (September 11, 1942)

Houses of refuge were established in and around Le Chambon-
sur-Lignon to feed, clothe, protect, and educate young children
and adolescents who, among others, had been brought out of internment camps, sometimes just before their parents were deported. By the middle of the Occupation, there were seven such houses in and near the village. Although Le Chambon-sur-Lignon was
relatively free from Nazi and Vichy raids, on the morning of June
29, 1943, disaster struck the house of refuge known as La Maison des Roches.[1] The building, located two kilometers from Le
Chambon-sur-Lignon, was formerly the fashionable Hôtel des
Roches. As of February 1942, financed by the Fonds européen de secours aux étudiants, it began to function as a house of refuge or sanc-

1. On the June 29, 1943, raid, see Gérard Bollon, "Contribution à l'histoire du
Chambon-sur-Lignon: Le Foyer Universitaire des Roches et la rafle de 1943," *Cahiers
de la Haute-Loire* (1996): 391–421; Georges Menut, "André Trocmé: un violent vaincu
par Dieu," 91–92; Pierre Fayol, *Le Chambon-sur-Lignon sous l'occupation (1940–1944)*
(Paris: L'Harmattan, 1990), 41–44.

tuary. Officially called Le Foyer universitaire des Roches, it housed in its thirty-odd rooms young male adults, mostly foreigners between the ages of twenty and thirty and mostly Jewish, some of whom had been interned in French-run concentration camps located in the southern part of the country. The majority of these young men were continuing their education in some capacity in Le Chambon-sur-Lignon. From February 1942 until March 1943, the house was directed by a retired couple, M. and Mme Pantet, who then asked to be replaced. At the request of his cousin, Pastor André Trocmé, Daniel Trocmé, already the director of Les Grillons, a house of refuge for young children, agreed to take on the additional position of director of La Maison des Roches, which then housed thirty refugees.

Daniel agreed to do so at a time when it was obvious to everyone in the area that the harboring of refugees was becoming a much more difficult and dangerous endeavor. André Trocmé notes in his "Mémoires" that "Daniel Trocmé, my cousin, accepted this difficult task when the raids of the *milice* [Vichy's political police and counterinsurgency unit] and those of the Gestapo were increasing."[2] As of November 1942, the Germans occupied the area around Le Chambon which, since June 1940, had been part of the Unoccupied Zone. Just one month before Daniel took over, the two pastors of the Reformed Church of France in Le Chambon-sur-Lignon, André Trocmé and Edouard Theis, were arrested along with the village's public school director, Roger Darcissac. Daniel and Doctor Roger Le Forestier went to Vichy on February 20 to plead for the release of the three men. National Protestant Federation president Marc Boegner also intervened on their behalf.

2. André Trocmé, "Mémoires," 395. Regarding the increasingly precarious nature of life for the refugees in Le Chambon-sur-Lignon in May and June 1943 and for slightly varying accounts on the June 29 raid of La Maison des Roches, see the following articles in Bolle et al., *Le Plateau Vivarais-Lignon: Accueil et Résistance 1939–1944*: Daniel Curtet, "Témoignage d'un ancien Pasteur," 54–67; Léon Chave, "Eléments de chronologie," 90–109; François Boulet, "Quelques éléments statistiques," 286–98; Antonio Plazas, "Remarques concernant les listes du registre de 'La Maison des Roches,'" 635–38; Jacques Poujol, "Les Victimes," 639–47.

At the beginning of May, six weeks or so after the men had returned to the village, two German *Feldgendarmes* came to La Maison des Roches and arrested an anti-Nazi German refugee named Ferber. He was given a letter to read and only enough time to pack his bags. Many sensed that the house had been targeted and that a larger roundup might be in the offing. Some students refused to spend the night there and slept at adjacent farms. But not all of them.[3] On the morning of June 29, 1943, some seven weeks after Ferber's arrest, the boarders of La Maison des Roches woke up at 6:30 to find the house surrounded by fifteen members of the Gestapo, a few of whom were wielding machine guns. The students were confined to the kitchen and interrogated individually in the director's office. There was no chance of escape into the woods. Around 7:30, the Gestapo was told that the director, Daniel Trocmé, had spent the night in Les Grillons, the other house he directed. Some of the soldiers went to Les Grillons, arrested Daniel, and brought him to La Maison des Roches. According to Magda Trocmé, as recorded in her husband's "Mémoires," the students at Les Grillons warned Daniel that the Gestapo was there to arrest him and urged him to hide in the woods. "I can't do that," Daniel responded, even though it appears that he might have escaped quite easily through the back door. "I'm responsible for Les Grillons and Les Roches."[4]

3. Basing his view partially on the research of Roger Debiève and Oscar Rosowsky, Serge Bernard claims that "the Resistance let André Trocmé know that a roundup at La Maison des Roches was imminent" and suggests that Trocmé "must have told his cousin, Daniel Trocmé, not to evacuate La Maison des Roches" (Serge Bernard, "La Construction de la mémoire légendaire," 73). Assuming that the Resistance did in fact warn the pastor about this imminent roundup, however, André Trocmé, who had been out of town for a month when the roundup actually took place, on June 29, 1943, might very well have warned the students about sleeping in La Maison des Roches because several students did in fact refuse to spend the night there. One wonders how the Resistance could have had this knowledge and, assuming they did, why they did not evacuate the home themselves when they discovered that Trocmé had been gone from the village for the entire month of June.

4. André Trocmé, "Mémoires," 396. Pages 396–99 of André Trocmé's "Mémoires" were written by Magda Trocmé. These pages cover the roundup at La Maison des Roches. Magda was in Le Chambon that day; André was not.

By 8:30, Daniel was assisting at the interrogations because he spoke German. When Magda managed to get into the house sometime around 10 a.m., Daniel urged her to go to the Hôtel du Lignon, where German soldiers convalesced, to have it verified that one of the arrested students had saved a German soldier from drowning. Magda did so and that student, Luis "Pepito" Gausachs, was released. Shortly after noon, those arrested were led outside; some were beaten; cries of "Schweine Juden" were heard. Eighteen students (fourteen foreigners and four Frenchmen) and Daniel Trocmé were loaded on trucks and taken away.[5]

All nineteen young men were deported. Seven survived. Six have never been accounted for. Georges Marx, Jacques Balter, Léonidas Goldenberg, Herbert Wollstein, and Charles Stern died in Auschwitz. On April 2, 1944, Daniel Trocmé died in the gas chamber at Maidanek. The last words Daniel spoke to any member of his family were said as he left La Maison des Roches the day of the raid, words addressed to Magda and recorded in English many years later in her interview in *The Courage to Care*: "Do not worry. Tell my parents that I was very happy here. It was the best time of my life. Tell them that I like traveling, that I go with my friends."[6]

⌣⟶

5. Ibid., 396–99. In his "Contribution à l'histoire du Chambon-sur Lignon" (pp. 408–11), Gérard Bollon provides the names of the nineteen young men arrested: a) those six who died in the gas chamber: Daniel Trocmé, Georges Marx, Jacques Balter, Léonidas Goldenberg, Herbert Wollstein, and Charles Stern; b) those six whose trace has been lost: Robert Kimmen, Frantz Weiss, Hermann Loewenstein, Camille Wouters, Alexandre De Haan, and Klaus Simon; and c) those seven who survived: Jean-Marie Schoen, André Guyonnaud, Jules Villasant-Dura, Félix Martin-Lopez, Sérafin Martin-Cayre, Pedro Moral-Lopez, and Antonio Perez.

6. Carol Rittner and Sondra Myers, *The Courage to Care*, 106.

Dear Parents: I am so sure that you are among those resisting [the German invasion], that I feel great pride and I believe that you have raised children who will be worthy of you.

Daniel Trocmé, Rome (May 20, 1940)[7]

Daniel spent half his life living at the Ecole des Roches at Verneuil-sur-Avre, which must not be confused with La Maison des Roches in Le Chambon-sur-Lignon. One could hardly overestimate the role that this atmosphere, and the family life that Daniel enjoyed in it with his eight siblings, played upon his intellectual and emotional development. Daniel's father, Henri Trocmé, born in Saint-Quentin in 1873 and raised in an austere Protestant milieu, decided after some tortured deliberations not to become a minister but to enter the teaching profession. In January 1902, he married Eve Rist and in October of that year began his career at the Ecole des Roches, which had recently been founded by the noted historian and sociologist Edmond Demolins. Henri Trocmé served as dean of that school until his death in 1944.[8]

The Ecole des Roches was an elegant and expensive English-style boarding school, one of the finest secondary schools in France. The students lived in houses supervised by married couples. For some forty years, Henri and Eve lived in the house named Les Sablons with a group of fifty male students aged eight to eighteen. Their nine children were raised in Les Sablons, where their father's motto, "Loyalty binds me" *(Loyauté me lie),* became the house's maxim and where their mother's personal ethic, "Live spiritually and love actively" *(Vis spirituellement et aime activement),* was equally influential.

---

7. "Daniel Geoffroy Trocmé (1912–1944)," 8. This is a nineteen-page typescript written by his brother Charles. A copy of this typescript is in my possession.

8. Both of Daniel Trocmé's parents died in the same year he did. A few months after Daniel's death, at the time of the Allies' advance in Normandy, Eve was killed instantly by shrapnel as she and her husband took shelter under a bridge on the campus of the Ecole des Roches. A short time later, on his way to church, Daniel's father, Henri, was run over and killed by an American jeep. André Trocmé, "Mémoires," 400.

At this school for the rich, Daniel received a privileged education. Born in 1912, he was eclectic by nature and interested in many subjects in the arts and sciences. At a young age he perfected his German when he spent seven months in Switzerland and later five months in Austria. He went on to do his best work in math and physics. After completing his *baccalauréat,* he took special courses in Paris for two years at two prestigious *lycées,* Louis-le-Grand and Henri IV. In December 1931, he fell ill, returned to Les Sablons, and spent months in bed with a serious heart disorder, pericarditis, that restricted his activities and perhaps even played a role in his ultimate fate.

In the fall of 1932, he returned to Paris to study at the Sorbonne for his *licence* in general physics, calculation of probability, and mathematical physics. He spent two more years there, making new friends from all over the world, doing a minimum amount of schoolwork, and hesitating to make a career decision. For the 1934–35 academic year, Daniel took a post at the Ecole Française of the American University in Beirut and in addition to his teaching duties, he traveled widely in Lebanon and Egypt.

In January 1935, in response to his father's suggestion that he return from Lebanon to teach at the Ecole des Roches, Daniel wrote: "Papa still proposes Les Roches, and I'm thinking about it, but I have my reservations. I still don't know who I am, or what I'm capable of, and I'd like to try my hand at several jobs before deciding definitively."[9] Four months later, toward the end of his academic year in Lebanon, still young at the age of 23, Daniel could not see himself tied down in a traditional career and preferred to continue to travel, teach, and make new friends: "I'd like to be completely free to say and do what I think and want. And that seems almost impossible to me in the majority of classic, bourgeois careers."[10]

There can be no doubt that his travels broadened his horizon

9. "Daniel Geoffroy Trocmé (1912–1944)," 5.
10. Ibid.

Daniel Trocmé in 1938, in a photo taken for his identification card for the Lycée Francais in Rome. *Courtesy of Robert Trocmé.*

and made him reconsider much of what he had previously taken for granted. As he explains in that May 24, 1935, letter to his parents: "I'm breaking free of Western Civilization. If you will, for me, it no longer represents civilization, but *a* civilization." He subjected the Christian religion to the same scrutiny: "I see what Christianity contains that is beautiful and true, and what is false and ugly in it." Without declaring war, Daniel is clearly liberating himself at once from the career that had been expected of him as a graduate of the prestigious Ecole des Roches and of the appropriate conservative religious sentiments that accompany such a career choice. "I want to continue to travel, to see new things, to liberate myself,"[11] he wrote and, fittingly, he accepted an interesting but very poorly paid job for the next academic year (1935–36) as director of the Foyer des Jeunes in Beirut.

During the 1936–37 academic year, Daniel was once again a student in Paris, this time at the Sorbonne, where he completed his teaching credentials. For the next three years, from 1937 to 1940, he served as professor of physics, chemistry, and natural sciences at the Lycée Français in Rome. Daniel returned to France during the terrible summer of 1940 and took a position as professor of math and physics at the Ecole des Roches, which had been temporarily relocated in the free zone at Maslacq in the Basses-Pyrénées. After spending two academic years there, he resigned in June 1942 without any set plans for the fall. A December 10, 1940, letter to his parents, in which he writes of himself and his students at the Ecole des Roches, indicates the path he was to take: "We see so much misery around us that we all think we are privileged."[12]

In July 1942, Daniel admitted that he was at a crossroads. He could return to the Ecole des Roches and perhaps eventually replace his father there. He also had a chance for a teaching job at the Lycée Français in Barcelona. On August 4, he told his parents that he had received "a firm proposition from André Trocmé: the direction of a house with twenty to twenty-five children of all nationalities aged twelve to eighteen, whose parents are currently interned, and who are studying at the Ecole Nouvelle Cévenole. It's an American foundation: I will be the headmaster as well as the academic director."[13] Shortly thereafter, the teaching job in Barcelona fell through and his parents suggested that he study for his doctorate.

11. Ibid., 6.   12. Ibid., 9.
13. Ibid., 11.

On September 11, in a powerful letter to his parents, Daniel announced his decision and his reasons for making that decision with such firm conviction that it seems to have emanated from a quasi-religious vocation or secular conversion:

> As of this morning, the die is cast . . . Le Chambon represents for me, first of all, an education . . . Then a kind of contribution to the reconstruction of our world . . . on the other hand, Le Chambon represents for me an affirmative response to a vocation, a rather intimate call and almost religious, or even completely religious in some respects. I will honestly be myself there, the future will tell me if I was equal to the task or not—and, what's more, will only tell me—because it's not a question here of success in the eyes of the world. Worldly wisdom directed me to the doctorate, or at least to Barcelona, or in any event to public teaching. Le Chambon means adventure . . . I have chosen this adventure, not because it's an adventure, but so that I would not be ashamed of myself.[14]

On October 1, 1942, Daniel took charge of Les Grillons and began what would be a nine-month personal commitment in Le Chambon that ultimately led to his deportation and death. His whole life, from the years at the Ecole des Roches to the recent seemingly aimless and undirected years in Paris and abroad, had been a preparation for his new work. In Le Chambon, he was in fact himself, and consequently, nothing he had ever done before brought him the same sense of fulfillment.

Daniel was responsible, at Les Grillons, for twenty children aged twelve to eighteen whose parents in many cases had been deported. The group's religious and ethnic diversity pleased Daniel's cosmopolitan nature. Among its nine girls and eleven boys were eleven

14. Letter from Daniel Trocmé to his parents (September 11, 1942). I first heard part of this extraordinary quotation in *Weapons of the Spirit*, before Robert Trocmé sent me copies of his brother's letters. From September 11, 1942, to the end of June 1943, Daniel wrote nine letters to his parents. His father copied these letters, which now cover twenty-five sheets of paper. The last of these letters is dated "End of March."

Catholics, eight Jews, one Protestant, six Spaniards, three Czechs, three Poles, one Austrian, one English child, four naturalized French children, and two illegitimate French children. Despite his heart ailment, Daniel worked long days with great intensity, often mending clothes, making soup, and repairing shoes with old automobile tires well into the night. A month after assuming his position, he wrote to his parents about his work: "up to now, it has absorbed me completely, and even beyond that." He is in charge of organizing everything, he wrote, obtaining false identity cards for his children, handling the finances, and dressing "all these kids from head to foot." To that end, after measuring them for their sizes, he made frequent trips, as the dead of winter drew near, to Le Puy, Lyon, Saint-Etienne, and to the Quakers in Marseille for warm coats, shoes, gloves, pants, galoshes, and, since the rooms were freezing, hot water bottles.

In addition to performing these and other time-consuming tasks for the physical well-being of his youngsters, Daniel wrote that he was also their "moral, intellectual, and spiritual director." He spent time doing math tutoring and substitute math teaching and made every effort to visit the children's parents who were in the internment camp at Gurs. His work was burdensome but also "interesting" and "useful," he told his parents; the youngsters in Les Grillons "intelligent and likeable," "very well-behaved and easygoing," "by and large wonderful." "I love them greatly," he wrote, "and furthermore, right now, as a group. But I rejoice in being able to know them better individually." "I adore them, and in return, I can say that they show me much affection." His youngsters helped him through the inevitable moments of solitude that he experienced in this context of genuine solidarity: "if I suffer on occasion from being alone, they amuse me rather than bother me."

Daniel often reassured his parents that he was healthy—"my health is excellent," "physically, I'm doing wonderfully"; and happy—"I am happy." And he discussed with them the heavy respon-

sibility he had assumed—"What will become of these children, uprooted since their birth, intelligent without egoism?" He knows he
is a necessary source of strength to them and has created a substitute family for them. He considers himself "the father, as I love to
say, of twenty children [who] have no mother." This responsibility
to his new family precluded his spending Christmas at home: "fourteen of the twenty children will remain at Les Grillons for the vacation, and I have to take care of them . . . We are truly a family—
without exaggeration, that's precisely the spirit that reigns here."
When, on March 25, he also took charge of La Maison des Roches,
his workload and responsibilities increased immeasurably, "insane
work, but insanely interesting," and the time for his children in Les
Grillons decreased accordingly: "Each day, my kids are more precious to me. It's heartbreaking for me to be able to spend so little
time with them from now on. They hold it against me, too."

Just a few days before the infamous roundup that would send
Daniel and others to their death, Daniel's brother François visited
him in Le Chambon-sur-Lignon. In a letter to his parents, dated,
coincidentally, June 29, 1943, the day of Daniel's arrest, François
told them that he had told his brother Charles that, when visiting
Daniel, "I will plead your case to Dani, arguing for his return to the
Ecole des Roches, explaining how desirable it is that tradition be
maintained and that papa's spirit continue unabated, all that you
know infinitely better than I." He also told them that he found Daniel "loved and esteemed . . . very happy, very useful . . . in the full
development of his personality . . . a director loving his responsibilities." Loving his responsibilities meant, of course, never abandon-
ing the children he now had:

> For his children who have passed from hand to hand, he wants to be
> a permanent father, not a transient one. He says . . . that for [these
> children] who have given him their confidence, as they would to a
> father, his departure, even if it is compensated by the arrival of a
> man of greater value, would in some way be another desertion which

could make some of them feel even more painfully their situation as abandoned children, tossed about by sometimes contrary but always unforeseen winds.[15]

While Daniel's choice was contrary to his parents' wishes, his letters allow us to see that he had been trying to show his parents all along that his new work did not constitute a break from them but was rather very closely connected to them. In his September 11, 1942, letter, in which he announced his decision to go to Le Chambon-sur-Lignon, he suggested that he was who he was because of them: "Another upbringing probably would have led to another decision." His parents actually were his models as he began his work in Les Grillons: "I think of you and imitate you constantly" (November 16, 1942). Later, he explained how much of what he does in Les Grillons—where the children have chosen the motto: "Act for all" *(Agir pour tous)* (March 11, 1943)—is similar to what they do at Les Sablons: "Many things come to me directly from you. Did I tell you that their notebook . . . carries the motto 'Loyalty Binds Me' [*Loyauté me lie*] above their signature? Our study is arranged exactly like that in Les Sablons, except for the table in the middle which does not exist (December 15, 1942) . . . Our Christmas resembles, in almost all of its details, the Christmases of Les Sablons" (January 1, 1943).

To a large extent, Daniel conceived of what he was doing in Le Chambon-sur-Lignon in the context of what his parents did in Les Sablons. Certainly his concept of service is radically different from that of his parents: "The Ecole des Roches does not represent God for me, and serving God does not mean, in my view, serving the Ecole des Roches" (September 11, 1942). Incapable of situating himself on the side of "the privileged," Daniel nonetheless felt that he was still working in his parents' spirit: "if I am not useful

15. Letter from François Trocmé to his parents (June 29, 1943). Excerpts that I quote from this letter are contained in unpublished Trocmé family documents, copies of which are in my possession.

to you in Le Chambon, at least I am faithful to you, perfectly faithful, that I know for sure" (September 11, 1942). André Trocmé confirmed Daniel's view when he wrote in his "Mémoires": "Daniel was a true product of the [Ecole des Roches] . . . totally devoid of selfishness and animated by a rigorous moral conscience. Poorly prepared to direct a home for adolescents, he nonetheless came through admirably."[16]

Dear Children of Les Grillons Big and Small: . . . I think that this separation actually brings us together, because now I understand a little better the adventures that so many of your parents have had. We will thus have many memories in common.

Daniel Trocmé, letter sent to his parents but addressed to the children of Les Grillons [17]

Daniel left Le Chambon-sur-Lignon on June 29, 1943. After nine months there, he had only nine more months to live. He was held in jail in Moulins until August 27, then transferred to Compiègne. He was deported in December 1943 to Buchenwald, then to Dora. A friend saw him there in January 1944. He was thin, weak, and very sick. His heart was obviously failing him and he had difficulty breathing. His friends in the camp tried to take care of him. He finally went to the infirmary and, more than likely, was sent to Maidanek along with 1,200 others on March 27. He died there, on the outskirts of Lublin, Poland, on April 2, 1944.[18] The letters and postcards he sent to his parents (one from Moulins, twelve from Compiègne, one from Buchenwald) on his nine-month death voyage tell us nothing new about him. They do, however, make it clear

16. André Trocmé, "Mémoires," 353.
17. Letter dated September 12, 1943. After Daniel's arrest, he sent fourteen letters and cards to his parents from jail and various camps. His father also copied these letters, which cover eighteen sheets of paper. Some of the letters were written on *papier hygiénique.*
18. "Daniel Geoffroy Trocmé (1912–1944)," 18–19.

that even under the worst possible conditions, Daniel continued to live according to the values and ideals that had originally accounted for his commitment in Le Chambon-sur-Lignon.

From the very beginning, Daniel's letters, often written on *papier hygiénique*, concern his basic material needs. Over the course of his imprisonment he asked his parents for food, vitamins, shoes, soap, clothing, toilet paper, anti-vermin lotion, pajama bottoms, a toothbrush, a nail brush, dry bread, dried vegetables, salt, and cigarettes. Somehow his parents managed to send him just about all these things and more (sugar, butter, honey). Daniel, for his part, not only shared them with those who received no packages, but encouraged his parents to have packages sent to students from La Maison des Roches who had not yet received anything. He also asks for books, and he reports on his extended readings: "Almost a book a day"; "Balzac, Vigny, Shakespeare, Aubry, Musset"; "a book on Dante, selections from Goethe . . . *Don Quixote, Madame Bovary, The Century of Louis XIV*"; "Dante's *Inferno* and *Man the Unknown*." Initially he seems to have done nothing but read. As of September 12, 1943, however, he envisioned more social activity: "I have continued to read a great deal these days and I am perhaps soon going to consider my vacation over, and take up some activity in the social life of the camp . . . Up to the present, I have almost exclusively lived in books."

To some extent, Daniel shared his fears with his parents but, as during his stay in Le Chambon-sur-Lignon, he seemed above all intent on assuring them that he was fine and undoubtedly would soon be released. "My morale is still good," he wrote from Moulins on August 13, 1943; "I hope to see you soon." Once at Compiègne— "infinitely better than Moulins . . . incredibly superior regarding freedom, food, and interest"—he met some old friends from the Ecole des Roches and began a "prison camp regime." He asked his parents to find out if Doctor Le Forestier might know of someone who could intervene on his behalf. He seemed to think that his case was "simplified by the fact that I believe myself unfit" due to his heart ailment. He was later judged, however, *"Gesund und lagerfähig"* ("healthy and campworthy"). Even though he continued to speak of his good health and his release ("morale excellent, health also"; "everything is going well here"; "my morale is getting better presently"), the real possibility of deportation does in fact surface in his letters home: "I barely escaped a departure for Germany which took Raoul Duval and Pastor Heuzé, as well as almost all my companions from Moulins." What never surfaces in his letters, however, not even once, is a complaint.

Daniel's greatest loss in the camps was that of human warmth. He constantly demanded news of his loved ones: "What I miss is news, yours and from Le Chambon. How is each little child in Les Grillons?" This quest for communication and communion is a constant leitmotif in the letters written after his arrest ("Send me a lot of news from everywhere, also from my kids at Les Grillons. The Ecole des Roches and your life are continually on my mind, as are my brothers and sisters.") and in his Christmas letter, full of gratitude for his parents and siblings, he reported thinking nostalgically of "those days of sweet family life."

During his internment, Daniel seemed much more worried about his youngsters in Les Grillons than himself. Maintaining a bond with them was foremost in his thoughts. Paradoxically, as the epigraph to this section indicates, he believed that this separation, by its nature, brought him spiritually closer to them. In any event, his letters are replete with references to them: "All my affection to my kids at Les Grillons"; "My thoughts go constantly to each of my kids who, without knowing it, are the ones who direct my reading. I hope to see them again soon, but I would like to be sure of seeing all of them."

Although forbidden to write anywhere but home, he wrote a letter to his youngsters on September 12, 1943, and mailed it to his parents. In it, he speaks of their reunion ("one of the most beautiful joys that I promise myself is seeing you again. It will be magnificent.") and of his pledge to them for after the war: "I will not leave you as long as it is in my power. You can be sure of that." He urged them, finally, to be courageous and generous and to persist together in the ideal of the family that they had created: "Try always to maintain self-control. Remain together . . . Our family is fragile . . . and so young."

In the last substantive letter he wrote before his death, his Christmas message, dated December 8, 1943, Daniel told his parents: "Since I am pseudo-head of a family, you can understand that the children of Les Grillons are particularly close to me in this season. Unfortunately, I can neither write to them individually nor collectively." He then asked his parents, as Christmas presents, to have 1,500 francs of his money distributed equally among the students of Les Grillons by Pastor Poivre, adding: "If I could have precise news about them, I would be infinitely happy."

You know the religious uncertainties of our son who was still trying to find himself. In giving his life, he found what he was looking for.

Daniel Trocmé's parents to André Trocmé[19]

Daniel's letters during the last eighteen months of his life are full of manifestations of his courage, generosity, and solidarity with his children and with humanity. They are replete with images that stress what ties human beings together rather than what divides them. On his travels to Beirut and Rome, as well as during his long stay in Paris, Daniel expanded himself by the discovery of other people who had alternate views of the human experience. At the same time, he never unlearned the lessons of loyalty, mutuality, and unselfish commitment that were those of Les Sablons.

Magda Trocmé is perhaps correct to claim that "Daniel did not call God God; he called God service, sympathy, devotion, sacrifice,

19. André Trocmé, "Mémoires," 400.

and enthusiasm for everything good and great, without theological links." He opposed religious factions, associated with "outsiders," and thought and acted in terms of the human family. This is why the community plays such a large role in his writings. His September 12, 1943, letter to his children at Les Grillons contains two striking images of community. The first is about its precariousness: "Our family is fragile . . . and so young that each one of us must take care of it as we would a young seedling, like one of those small fir shoots found on the road to Les Grillons, and that each of us takes care several times each day not to damage." The second underscores the persistence of community by the evocation of a joyful communal celebration for a group of friends with shared memories, even if in a weakened state in a concentration camp in Compiègne during an evening meal that might very well serve as a prelude to a morning of deportation and death:

> Therefore, tomorrow night, we will have a dinner of the former students of the Ecole des Roches, outside or in room 9 of building A3 . . . The menu has not been completely fixed; but the main dish will be soup offered by the French Red Cross, garnished if possible with sardines, meat, apples, gingerbread, cookies and jams. In any event, we will do our best. There will probably even be a half glass of wine (Red Cross) and cigarettes. We are all rejoicing greatly.

This beacon, Daniel Trocmé, was right to affirm that Le Chambon-sur-Lignon from 1939 to 1944 was "a kind of contribution to the reconstruction of our world." President Jacques Chirac made the same point in his speech there on July 8, 2004. Sixty years after Daniel's death, when the United Nations has designated the decade 2001–10 "the Decade for a Culture of Peace and Nonviolence for the Children of the World," it is a good time to recall Daniel's commitment to those values at Les Grillons and La Maison des Roches, where he earned his doctorate in humane actions. At a time of extensive collaboration with the Nazis, he and others like him maintained the honor of France. On August 3, 1946, he was award-

תעודת כבוד
ATTESTATION

וזאת לתעודה שבישיבתה	Le présent Diplôme atteste qu'en
ביום ט"ז אדר ב' תשל"ו	sa séance du 13 Mars 1976
והליטה הועדה	la Commission des Justes près
לציון חסידי אומות העולם	l'Institut Commémoratif des
שליד רשות הזכרון יד ושם,	Martyrs et des Héros Yad Vashem
על יסוד עדויות	a décidé, sur foi de témoignages
שהובאו לפניה,	recueillis par elle, de rendre
לתת כבוד ויקר ל	hommage à feu

דניאל טרוקמה הצנוע
DANIEL TROCMÉ

על' אשר בעיתות השואה	qui au péril de sa vie a
באירופה שם נפשו בכפו	sauvé des Juifs pendant
להצלת יהודים נרדפים	l'époque d'extermination;
מיד רודפיהם	de lui décerner la
ולהעניק לו את המדליה	Médaille des Justes
לחסידי אומות העולם	et de l'autoriser à planter
ולהרשות לו לנטוע עץ	un arbre en son nom
בשמו בשדרת חסידי	dans l'Allée des Justes
אומות העולם	sur le Mont du Souvenir
על הר הזכרון בירושלים.	à Jérusalem:
ניתן היום ה כסליו תשל"ז	Fait à Jérusalem, Israël,
בירושלים, ישראל	le 30 Novembre 1976

Yad Vashem certificate declaring Daniel Trocmé "Righteous among the Nations" (1976). *Courtesy of Robert Trocmé.*

ed the Medal of the French Resistance. On March 18, 1976, he was deemed "Righteous among the Nations of the World," and a carob tree was planted in his name along the Avenue of the Righteous at Yad Vashem in Jerusalem. Today, in front of La Maison des Roches, a plaque with a white dove reads:

> Here on June 29, 1943, the Gestapo arrested 19 students [actually 18] and their director. They were deported to the death camps. They all lived out an ideal of justice and fraternity. "Those who believed in God and those who didn't."
>
> They will remain forever engraved in our memory.
>
> Antonio Plazas[20]

20. Antonio Plazas, who was living in La Maison des Roches when it was raided, is the only commentator who claims there were twenty young men arrested there on June 29, 1943. He does not provide names. He gives only the nationality of those arrested: "5 Spaniards, 4 Frenchmen, 2 young men from Luxemburg, 2 Dutchmen, 2 Germans, 2 Belgians, 1 Austrian, 1 Romanian, 1 Pole." "Remarques concernant les listes du registre de 'La Maison des Roches,'" in Bolle et al., *Le Plateau Vivarais-Lignon,* 636. See footnote 5 in this chapter for the nineteen names provided by Gérard Bollon.

3 ⌣

Madeleine Dreyfus
Righteous Jew

Above all, she loved human relations.

Annette Davis

*How this young mother from a bourgeois family transformed herself into
a character from a war novel is a mystery to me. To her also, I think. . . .*

Michel Dreyfus

Madeleine Dreyfus[1] was one of the Oeuvre de secours aux enfants (OSE) Jewish fieldworkers who placed children in homes and
institutions in the south of France. More specifically, she escorted
children from Lyon to the area of Le Chambon-sur-Lignon. Born
Madeleine Kahn,[2] the first of five children, in 1909, into an atheis-

---

1. I cite numerous unpublished family texts, written primarily by Madeleine and
her husband, Raymond, whose lengthy biographical memoir about his wife, "Ecoute:
une 'psy' selon Alfred Adler," was extremely valuable. I also quote memoirs written by
two of their children, Michel Dreyfus (1934–2003) and Annette Davis, and unpublished professional manuscripts written by Madeleine.

2. *Our* Madeleine Dreyfus must not be confused with the Resistance fighter
named Madeleine Dreyfus Lévy, the granddaughter of the famous Captain Alfred Dreyfus. After the Vel d'Hiv roundup in July 1942, she joined the Combat underground resistance group. She was arrested on November 3, 1943, and sent to Auschwitz, where
she died of typhus in January 1944 at the age of twenty-five. On her life, see Michael
Burns, *Dreyfus, a Family Affair: From the French Revolution to the Holocaust* (New York:

tic family of Jewish origins, she was deeply loved by a father whom she adored but, at the same time, was the victim of her mother's enduring hostility, which caused her long-term anguish and made her crave her mother's approbation. During her youth, she never experienced any feelings of solidarity with what one might term "the Jewish community." From her earliest days, her friends were of all religions and of diverse political opinions. She often spent vacations with her best friend, Suzanne Tourneur, a practicing Catholic.

After having studied at the Lycée Jules Ferry in Paris, Madeleine received her *baccalauréat* degree in 1927, at that time a relatively rare achievement for a woman. She then earned a diploma in stenography and worked for a year as an English-French bilingual secretary in an import-export firm. Shortly thereafter, while working for the designer and fine-books binder Rose Adler, she discovered the vast Parisian Surrealist milieu, where she found herself very much at home in a group of social nonconformists, such as Jean Cocteau, André Breton, and other intellectuals. She later maintained correspondence with Pierre Mendès-France, Roger Martin du Gard, Robert Aron, and Claude Lévi-Strauss.

When she was not yet engaged at the age of 23, Madeleine's parents arranged for her to meet Raymond Dreyfus. Madeleine and Raymond shared an intense interest in contemporary French literature and the artistic life in Paris and were married in March 1933, ominously on the very day Hitler came to power in Germany. Thanks to her cousin, Andrée Hauser, Madeleine became passionately interested in psychology and its practical application. She had the good fortune of meeting and studying with the Viennese refugee Sophie Lazarsfeld, a student and disciple of Alfred Adler. Sophie and Madeleine became lifelong friends. While Madeleine's new professional interests were blossoming, she gave birth to two sons, Michel in 1934, and Jacques in 1937.

Harper Collins, 1991), 428–31; 480–83; and James Carroll, *Constantine's Sword. The Church and the Jews: A History* (New York: Houghton Mifflin Company, 2001), 468–71.

Madeleine Dreyfus in 1943. *Courtesy of Michel Dreyfus.*

When the war broke out in 1939, Raymond was drafted into the military. He was discharged in July 1940. During that time, Madeleine taught elementary school for ten months in the Vexin, a region in Normandy. In October 1941, when Raymond lost his job in Paris because of the anti-Semitic laws, they settled in Lyon in the Unoccupied Zone. Soon after her arrival, Andrée Hauser, who was about to leave for Brazil, asked Madeleine if she would replace her as the psychologist at the medical-social center of OSE. Madeleine did so, and gave educational and psychological consultations to troubled Parisian students whose families had taken refuge in Lyon. While on a short vacation in August 1942 at Saint Bonnet de Joux, a small village in the heart of Burgundy, Madeleine received a telegram from Elizabeth Hirsch of OSE urging her to return immediately. She took the next train back to Lyon, where she agreed to become part of an illegal rescue mission. Now that Jewish children were being rounded up even in the still-unoccupied zone, this was a rather precarious endeavor. For Madeleine, it was no longer a matter of simply helping children adjust to extremely demanding circumstances. It was a question of saving lives. As Madeleine put it, she now had to transform "the children of Katz into the children of Durand-Dupont" and find hiding places for them. Her fellow Jewish rescuer Denise Siekierski remarks that this was accomplished at great personal risk: "We lived clandestinely under the constant menace of the Gestapo."[3]

Assisted by Marthe Sternheim and eventually also by Margot Kohn, Madeleine worked out of OSE headquarters on the rue Montée des Carmélites in Lyon, where she continued OSE's official and legal work of helping needy Jewish families. At the same time, she began her clandestine work, which consisted of having false identity papers and ration cards made and of hiding Jewish children and some Jewish adults. While canvassing religious and lay institutions in the Lyon area to find places to hide Jewish children, Madeleine met the retired teachers M. and Mme Paul Jouve d'Oullins, who sent her to their relatives in Le Chambon-sur-Lignon. This was a godsend. She now assumed responsibility for the Lyon/Le Chambon-sur-Lignon area link in the Garel Network and sought places of refuge in this mostly Protestant countryside for her Jewish children.[4]

3. Letter to author, September 14, 1999.
4. The collection edited by Pierre Bolle et al., *Le Plateau Vivarais-Lignon: Accueil*

Several times a month, accompanied by a very small group of children (aged anywhere from eighteen months to sixteen years), Madeleine would take the train from Lyon to Saint-Etienne where she would transfer to *"le tortillard"* (the local steam engine train) to Le Chambon-sur-Lignon. Sometimes these children had been given to her by their parents. Just as often, they had managed to escape at the time of their parents' arrest. Although in almost all cases the children had false Aryan identity papers, Madeleine did not. She had to take control of these mostly foreign children to get them through police inspections in the train stations and on the trains. She had to keep them from speaking Polish, German, or Yiddish, and make sure that they called their friends by their French names.

From September or October 1942 to November 1943, Madeleine made these trips to find shelter for well over one hundred Jewish children. She returned often to visit the children she had placed, to take them clothing, medicine, food tickets, and whenever possible letters from their parents, who, for safety reasons, never knew where their children were hidden. As her son Michel notes: "She was animated by a relentless ardor and vitality." Madeleine did all she could to help the children adjust to their new situation. OSE gave money to help the farmers who housed the children but, according to Madeleine, "The money for room and board paid by OSE was minimal . . . and clearly insufficient to cover the expenses incurred by the children."

Normally, when asked to speak about her work on the plateau, Madeleine spoke about those who helped her. She pointed out that her first contacts in Le Chambon-sur-Lignon were with André and Magda Trocmé and that she was also greatly indebted to the other Protestant pastors on the plateau, to Roger Darcissac, the director

---

et Résistance 1939–1944, is helpful regarding how Madeleine did what she did on the plateau. Particularly useful are Sabine Zeitoun, "Accueil d'enfants Juifs de l'Oeuvre de Secours aux Enfants (O.S.E.) par le Plateau Vivarais-Lignon," 221–26; Michel Fabréguet, "Les réfugiés et l'accueil," 129–50; and Madeleine Dreyfus, "L'O.S.E.," 216–20.

of the public school in Le Chambon-sur-Lignon, to La Cimade, and to Mme Mairesse, a young war widow who lived in Le Mazet-Saint-Voy and regularly took Jewish refugee children to Pastor Curtet in Fay-sur-Lignon.

No one receives more praise, however, and more space in her accounts, than Mme Léonie Déléage and her eldest daughter, Eva (now Eva Phillit of Saint-Etienne). Mme Déléage, from Les Tavas, was the regional *correspondante* of the Garel Network. But, for Madeleine, she was "much more than that . . . she was our devoted friend who herself contacted the families most likely to help hide these Jewish children pursued by the Gestapo." When Madeleine arrived in Le Chambon-sur-Lignon, she was normally met by Eva. They left the children at the Hôtel May and then went from farm to farm looking for places of refuge, many of which had been prepared in advance by Mme Déléage. The children were placed in families that housed and protected them from the French police and the Germans who were searching for them. Whenever possible, well in advance of roundups the children were hidden in the surrounding woods. The older people stayed in their homes and played dumb. Madeleine loved to tell the story of Mme Déléage who, when questioned by German soldiers and asked if there were Jews in the area, responded: "Jews, what does that mean 'Jews?'" Raymond Dreyfus also singles out Mme Déléage for special praise. In one of his unpublished manuscripts, entitled "Mes souvenirs du Chambon au cours des années 1943–44," he tells of a visit to her home sometime during the winter of 1943–44. In addition to finding places of shelter for the Jewish children, Mme Déléage hid numerous children in her own home, which, in Raymond's view on that snowy day, "overflowed with children from everywhere in Europe." For Raymond, Mme Déléage was not only "characterized by an uncommon goodness and simplicity" but was also, for Madeleine, "the pivot of her rescue activity."

Madeleine kept a notebook with the names of many of the children she had placed and those of the families sheltering them, along with the things they requested she bring on her next visit. "How would I have been able to remember all that, but what a lack of prudence," she writes. She makes the same remarks about her notebook in *Weapons of the Spirit,* which contains the only filmed interview with her. Fortunately, the notebook was never seized by the authorities. Today, a copy of it is on display in Le Chambon-sur-Lignon. In Madeleine's notebook, Annik Flaud discovered a copy, written in shorthand, of part of a pastoral message from Cardinal Gerlier, archbishop of Lyon, that was read on September 6 from the pulpit of the Catholic churches in that diocese.[5] The message was an affirmation of basic human rights for all human beings and of the sanctity of the family. André Trocmé and Edouard Theis had asked Madeleine to get them a copy of it. Perhaps nothing symbolizes the ecumenical nature of the whole rescue endeavor better than this Jewish woman, at the request of Protestant pastors, taking a Catholic archbishop's pastoral message to the plateau Vivarais-Lignon.

In November 1942, Madeleine was pregnant with her third child, Annette. This may have slowed her down, but it did not stop her: "I was pregnant," she wrote, "and continued my work as well as I could." Annette was born in Lyon on August 29, 1943. "Very shortly thereafter," writes Raymond, "my wife resumed her trips back and forth between Lyon and Le Chambon." At the same time, in September 1943, Raymond's sister-in-law and two of her children were arrested and deported. Very soon thereafter, Raymond begged Madeleine to stop her illegal work: "I begged my wife to stop this dangerous activity now that she was responsible for three small children, two months, six, and nine years of age, all without false papers." For her part, Madeleine asked Raymond to wait a bit longer since there was no one to replace her. As she explained years later: "It was difficult to convince me, but somewhere around Novem-

5. "They [Trocmé and Theis] asked Madeleine to transcribe the text in shorthand in her 'little notebook.'" Letter of Annik Flaud to Nelly Trocmé Hewett, November 24, 1998. A copy of this letter is in my possession.

ber 10th, I saw Andrée Salomon and told her she would eventually have to replace me but there was no rush."

On November 23,[6] Madeleine received a phone call from the father of a child she had hidden at the Institut des sourds-muets (School for Deaf-Mutes) at Villeurbanne, which served as a *lieu de transit,* or transfer point, where children were sometimes lodged before being dispersed into homes, religious institutions, or more generally into Switzerland. The caller, M. Kadous, was distraught because he had heard that there was going to be a Gestapo raid at the Institute. Madeleine called the Institute and asked if "the Durand children" were okay and if they needed anything. The woman at the other end of the line responded: "It is difficult to answer you on the phone; you should come by the school right away." It was impossible for Madeleine to know that her respondent was being held at gunpoint and had been instructed to respond in that manner.

Madeleine, however, knew something was wrong. The woman whom Anny Latour refers to as "the fearless Madeleine Dreyfus"[7] went home, said nothing about this to her husband, collected all her "compromising papers," including her "little notebook," put them in a trunk in a warehouse in her neighborhood, took the streetcar to Villeurbanne, and walked into a trap that had been set for the director of the Institute, M. Pellet, who was an important member of the Resistance (in the Marco-Polo Network). He was soon captured and executed.

As Madeleine waited with others to be questioned, she realized that, since she did not have false papers, they would immediately see "Dreyfus (née Kahn)" with the word "Jew" marked on her papers. Much worse, they would also find her address. Fearful for her husband and children, she had to act before they found out who she

6. Only in her published article "L'O.S.E.," in *Le Plateau Vivarais-Lignon,* 219, does Madeleine give the date as November 27. All of her unpublished writings and those of her husband give November 23.

7. Anny Latour, *La Résistance juive en France (1940–1944)* (Paris: Stock, 1970), 188.

was. She asked to be allowed to go home to breastfeed her three-month-old daughter. When they refused, she insisted that they allow her to call home so that her daughter would be given a bottle. She knew she would have only one call and decided to warn as many people as possible. She dialed M. Daltroff at the Union général des Israélites de France (U.G.I.F.), the National Jewish Council created to coordinate Jewish social and philanthropic organizations in the occupied and unoccupied zones. Here is what M. Daltroff heard before an irate Gestapo member grabbed the phone and hung it up: "Madeleine Dreyfus here. Would you kindly inform my family that I have been arrested by the Gestapo and will not be home to feed my daughter?" Wanting to know that her family was safe, a few hours later she once again insisted on going home to feed her daughter. This time those in charge acquiesced. Accompanied by a Gestapo officer whom she could not shake on the way, she entered an apartment that had obviously been vacated in a hurry. She had at least the consolation of knowing that her family had gotten the word. As she gathered some clothes together, the telephone rang. It was her mother. "Go away . . . Leave . . . all of you," she told her.

Raymond and others did all they could to have Madeleine liberated. They tried every connection, pulled every string, but to no avail. Her work would go on nonetheless. The future assistant mayor of Jerusalem, André Chouraqui, replaced her at OSE in Lyon and in the Garel Network. Her family was also safe. Raymond took Jacques and Michel to Le Chambon-sur-Lignon, where they were hidden in the home of Mme Lebrat in the hamlet of La Bourghea, while Madeleine's mother took in Annette, and her sister Martine became, in Raymond's words, Annette's "true substitute mother."

For Madeleine, humiliation and abuse began immediately. Her interrogation took place late at night on the day of her arrest. Both Raymond and Michel Dreyfus say she was interrogated by Klaus Barbie. Madeleine does not seem quite sure: "Perhaps it was Barbie. In any event, it was one of his henchmen because he directed all operations at that time in that sector." Without false papers, she was immediately identified as Jewish. Here is her account:

> —"A Jew. Are you a Jew?"
> —"Yes," I answered calmly.
> Then he literally began to foam at the mouth, sporting an expression of extreme disgust. A filthy beast would not have had a more horrible effect upon him. Undoubtedly in order to "cleanse" me of this disgrace, he threw the contents of a carafe of water in my face. It made me smile.
> —"You'll no longer be laughing when I send you to the Russian front."

Madeleine was sent to Fort Montluc in Lyon where she spent over two months in the "Jewish women's dormitory," from whose window she witnessed the execution of many Jewish and non-Jewish resisters. Fortunately for her, the Gestapo never found out about her illegal activities. For them, her only crime was the unpardonable one of being Jewish. The absence of news about her family caused her intolerable grief: "I was afraid that they might also have been arrested. I thought I heard babies crying, that could only have been my little Annette (three months old), or children crying and I thought of my two boys." In a sonnet from his *La Liberté guide nos pas*[8] that could have been written for Madeleine Dreyfus, Resistance poet Pierre Emmanuel depicts a prisoner at Fort Montluc struggling to make contact with his loved ones even as he himself cannot be seen clearly by them:

FORT MONTLUC

A vague terrain where the blue child plays with the grass
the woman and under her folds of courage her fruit,
another woman—heart burning her awkward black dress—
and near them the focus of their looks your friend

8. Pierre Emmanuel, *La Liberté guide nos pas* (Paris: Seghers, 1946), 64.

All the force of their eyes penetrates
the meager obscurity beyond the prison bars. Two faces
yours, that of the young father. They smile at us
with an invisible smile that tingles on our temples

So intensely does your blood run through us. I see you
no! I scrutinize a far off oval of half-light
where glass flies in bits in the setting sun

Without a gesture, we follow the flight of captive hands
they cry out on the sea, and we cry! The child
dares a kiss toward you, swallow! for a long time.

At the end of January 1944, Madeleine was transferred to Drancy where she spent the next four months. When she arrived at 2 a.m., she had the enormous good fortune to be greeted by André Ullmo, an old friend, lawyer, and underground worker in Lyon, who was now one of the prisoners in charge of reception and registration. Without him, Madeleine would have been sent to Auschwitz two days after her arrival at Drancy. He classified her as the wife of a prisoner of war because, at that time, such persons were not being deported. She invented a number for her prisoner of war husband, a camp where he was held, and a three-year-old daughter who was dependent upon her.

Anny Latour notes that even from Drancy, Madeleine managed to save more Jewish children: "Knowing the danger that seemed imminent for a group of Jewish children in the vicinity of Grenoble, she succeeded, from Drancy itself, in sounding the alert. Thanks to her, the children would be saved."[9] The children whom she could not help were those who came to Drancy. It was particularly painful for her to see the children from Isieu arrive at Drancy without being able to save them from Auschwitz. She had placed some of them in that OSE home herself, "two little girls and two boys named Balsam," she reports.

9. Anny Latour, *La Résistance juive en France*, 188.

Also from Drancy, suddenly fearful that Le Chambon with its large concentration of Jewish refugees might no longer be safe, she managed to get a letter to her mother with a coded message to encourage her husband to have Michel and Jacques smuggled into Switzerland. The message, "The boys must stop eating ham *("jambon")*, as our Alsatian friends say," stumped everyone until one of their Alsatian friends, Marthe Sternheim, read it out loud. Suddenly *"jambon"* sounded enough like "Chambon" (where the boys were hidden) for the family to understand.[10] Raymond contacted Germaine Masour, who made arrangements with La Cimade and the boys made it safely into Switzerland, where they remained in a children's home until the end of the war. Years later, reflecting on his mother's arrest and various incarcerations, Michel wrote: "From her prisons, she watched over us."

Ultimately, even the wives of the prisoners of war were deported. They came from camps all over France and from other detention centers in the Parisian area: "they arrived at Drancy," Madeleine wrote, "from various camps in France: Pithiviers, Beaune-La-Rolande, and 'camps' in Paris at the Gare d'Austerlitz, at Lévitan's on Rue Bassano, and undoubtedly elsewhere as well." At the end of May 1944, Madeleine was deported with them to Bergen-Belsen, a concentration camp without gas chambers near Celle in northwest Germany. On April 15, 1945, it was the first camp liberated by Western Allied forces, but not before some forty thousand inmates had died there of starvation and disease. As her train passed through Belgium, Madeleine, always anxious to reassure her family, threw a short note addressed to them out of the train. Thanks to Belgian and French railway workers, it made its way to them. In it, Madeleine assured them that she was full of hope and begged them to exercise prudence—"a prudence," her husband remarked over forty years later,

10. Madeleine records this incident herself. In letters to me, both Michel Dreyfus (letter of April 27, 2001) and Lili-Elise Garel (letter of December 17, 1999) comment on it in some detail.

"that she had hardly ever practiced for herself in the course of her clandestine activities, since she gave such priority to rescue activity."

Nothing characterizes Madeleine's writings more than self-effacement. When asked to talk about her work in Le Chambon-sur-Lignon, she normally spoke or wrote only about those who helped her place the children. The same modesty and concern for others also marks her writings about her various incarcerations:

[About Fort Montluc]

Of course, it was no picnic but what painful experiences I had there are hardly worth relating when one thinks about the horrors that took place at the same time in the cellars on Avenue Berthelot, at Saint Genis-Laval, and other places around Lyon.

[About Drancy]

Once again, I'll skip over the details of my stay there. But I saw some friends from OSE pass through: Simone Kahn, arrested in Grenoble on the Place de la Madeleine. Simone agreed to take responsibility for two little girls during the trip. We didn't know, we who asked her to do so, that, in a way, we condemned her to death. How could we have possibly imagined the gas chambers?

[About Bergen-Belsen]

I will not dwell on this "stay," which lasted eleven months.

[About the entire experience]

Fort Montluc, Drancy, Bergen-Belsen. They are hardly pleasant places; but I came back. Therefore, I won't complain. Too many among us were arrested, deported, and did not return. What horrors I lived through and skirted: and I rejoiced that thanks to the devotion of all our friends in the Haute-Loire region a good number of children—and adults—were able to avoid all of that.

It is, then, almost exclusively through the writings of others that we learn of Madeleine's activities in prison and in the camps. Her husband and her son Michel stress her determination in Bergen-Belsen, where she spent eleven months, to maintain her dignity in a situation (hunger, sleeplessness, dysentery, typhus, constant fear, and depression) specifically designed to destroy it. Raymond mentions an incident in which a German soldier on guard in a watchtower tossed her a piece of bread: "this soldier, perhaps an S.S., threw her a piece of bread that she refused to pick up, even as hunger dominated her being and condemned her to death." "Another [German soldier]," writes Michel, "offered her food to make love. She refused."[11]

Even in this situation, Madeleine was, as always, concerned with the well-being of others. By sending two letters for her family to Raymond's brother in Switzerland, she managed to let them know she was still alive. Characteristically, Raymond notes, there was "no detail whatsoever about the horror into which the camp had plunged." In Bergen-Belsen, she ministered to her fellow prisoners: "I was trying to raise the morale of my companions." Many others have testified to her success in this endeavor. Raymonde Kanters spoke to Madeleine's husband about "daily delousing sessions during which Madeleine encouraged her companions, by her example, to get rid of the vermin that transmitted typhus and was the cause, along with hunger, of the great majority of deaths." Raymond Dreyfus says he was often told that "thanks to Madeleine's incentive and example . . . numerous human lives were saved."

In a letter to me, Lili-Elise Garel, who was arrested by the Gestapo at the same time as Madeleine, notes that "Madeleine, according to what I found out, was always ready to help others in Bergen-Belsen. I know that a woman gave her a beautiful pair of scissors to give to her family, if Madeleine survived. In the camp, Madeleine would have been able to exchange these scissors for bread, but her moral standards forbade her to do so."[12] One of the most striking indications that Madeleine was greatly trusted by the other prison-

11. Letter from Michel Dreyfus to author, October 23, 1999.
12. Letter from Lili-Elise Garel to author, December 17, 1999.

ers is the fact that she was chosen to divide a hard-boiled egg into fifteen pieces.[13] "I still have the taste of that fifteenth of the hard-boiled egg in my mouth," she wrote many years later. Her son concludes that, during her eleven months in Bergen-Belsen, Madeleine "aroused in those who came in contact with her respect and admiration. . . . Her companions found in her a model and a comfort."[14]

There is one text, however, in which Madeleine does speak about her experiences in Bergen-Belsen. Undated and entitled "Problèmes psycho-sociologiques concernant les camps de déportés,"[15] this twenty-six-page study was, according to Raymond, presented to the Faculté des Lettres de Paris sometime around 1950. A research paper with many quotations from Bettelheim, Minkowski, Abel, Bondy, Sherif, Frankl, and several others, it is, in the main, a probing study of the dilemma faced by deported persons in the camps, and an analysis of how one survived a dreadful situation specifically designed to spread terror in the overall population and to crush individuals by slowly destroying everything that made them human.

What is of great interest here is how this text sheds light on the normally reticent Madeleine's experience in Bergen-Belsen. At the very beginning of her presentation, she admits to having been tempted to call the professor in charge, M. Durandin, "to tell him that I had broken my leg." It was very painful for her to look backward: "I thought I had done a much better job of coming to terms with all those things . . . I was deluding myself." In addition, she seemed to feel that she would be betraying her fellow prisoners if

13. The story of the hard-boiled egg is mentioned by Madeleine and corroborated by Michel.

14. Letter from Michel Dreyfus to author, October 23, 1999.

15. This was not among the papers sent to me initially by Michel Dreyfus. Since Raymond Dreyfus mentions it in his long account of Madeleine's life, however, I asked Michel if he would try to locate it. We were both grateful to Michel's nephew, Jean-Pierre Dreyfus, son of Michel's brother, Jacques (1937–1963), who found a copy.

she were somehow to make their suffering into a means to an end: "what was most unpleasant to me was the impression of analyzing all this suffering, all these people who died and, in short, making objects of study out of them."

Regarding her own experience, during the winter of 1944–45, she consumed between six hundred and seven hundred calories a day, and whereas there were sixty women living in her barracks when she arrived in Bergen-Belsen, within a few weeks six hundred women occupied the same space. Most haunting of all throughout her narration are the effects, both physical and psychological, of prolonged hunger. Before giving any personal examples, she cites a French psychologist named Bondy, who observed that "the most important thing became finding something to eat and drink. When they brought the food, an excitement occurred that was absolutely comparable to that of animals." She then notes: "I remember, for my part, having thoroughly enjoyed the rutabaga peelings left by a friend." Seeing herself reacting in such a way eventually brought on feelings of deep self-degradation. On another occasion, when a group of women arrived from Drancy with cans of food, her desire to eat was so overwhelming that she broke down, wondering how she could have been brought so low: "I remember having cried when realizing the intense desire I had to eat a piece of ham that was being enjoyed on the opposite bed. How had I gotten to that point?" These passages recall another that appears only in Raymond's account: taken by train from Bergen-Belsen during the last days of the war, Madeleine and others walked the fields looking for something to eat, anything at all, "in pursuit of any grass, any dandelion, to make some kind of salad." One day, she and her friend Marcelle came upon a railway workers' shack that had a pot on the stove with bones in it that had been used to make soup. Madeleine told Raymond: "Marcelle and I threw ourselves on those bones to try to find some nourishment in them, to satisfy this hunger that gnawed at us for so long, and even more so since the train had left, twelve long days before. Animals . . . I felt then what an animal can experience sucking, biting the bones of an animal it has just killed."

Although Madeleine notes: "I saw women in our camp throw their bread over the barbed wires to those unfortunate ones from Auschwitz who seemed even more hungry than we were," she makes it clear that gratuitous acts of generosity, "especially between strangers," were more or less nonexistent. In most cases, however, survival was contingent upon selective camaraderie—"A loner cannot survive." Very small groups of three or four women would stay together and in these groups they were able to help one another maintain morale ("those who lost their morale died quickly") and their humanity. They shared food, helped each other cope, assumed social roles, made an effort to speak about art and literature, and reassured themselves that they were still human beings. All that these women did together for their mutual survival justifies Madeleine's reflection: "One is really defeated only when one willingly surrenders."

Historians are coming to realize that Jewish resistance, in all its manifestations, was a widespread phenomenon.

Robert Rozett

Perhaps it was permissible in 1963, when Hannah Arendt published *Eichmann in Jerusalem,* to offer idle speculations regarding Jewish cooperation during the Holocaust. Our knowledge of this horrific event at that time was absolutely minimal compared to what we know today. Heavily influenced by Raul Hilburg's *The Destruction of the European Jews,* published in 1961, Arendt writes:

Wherever Jews lived, there were recognized Jewish leaders, and this leadership, almost without exception, cooperated in one way or another, for one reason or another, with the Nazis. The whole truth was that if the Jewish people had really been unorganized and leaderless, there would have been chaos and plenty of misery but the total number of victims would hardly have been between four and a half and six million people.[16]

Thirty-eight years later, however, in *Rethinking the Holocaust,* Yehuda Bauer points out that not only were the Jewish Councils "in many of the Polish and Lithuanian ghettos . . . not asked for and did not deliver lists of Jews," but also "many of the Soviet territories had no Judenräte [Jewish Councils], and the destruction was even more efficient there than in Poland." Finally, as Bauer also reports, in many smaller places, the Judenräte refused to cooperate in any way whatsoever.[17]

In many areas of Holocaust research, the "whole truth," to use Arendt's phrase, has become much more nuanced over the years. In chapters 6 ("Jewish Resistance—Myth or Reality?") and 7 ("Unarmed Resistance and Other Responses"), Bauer helps unsettle entrenched assumptions regarding Jewish inaction and cooperation with the Nazis. Blanket statements concerning "Jewish passivity" fly in the face of the totality of research and constitute perhaps the last great myth of the Holocaust. Hundreds of thousands of Jews resisted the Nazis in a variety of ways, and even if we can certainly still speak of passivity among Jews and other victims of the Nazis, it is no longer responsible to speak of "Jewish passivity" to imply a uniform mode among all Jews in the way Arendt speaks of Jewish leaders in the ghettos. Furthermore, as Berel Lang points out, given the "systematic brutality of the Nazi regime," resistance on all fronts, even in "circumstances much more favorable to resistance than those in which the Jews found themselves," was "far from common." Lang underscores the fact that three million Soviet

16. Hannah Arendt, *Eichmann in Jerusalem: A Report on the Banality of Evil* (New York: Penguin, 1963), 125.

17. Yehuda Bauer, *Rethinking the Holocaust* (New Haven, Conn.: Yale University Press, 2001), 77–78. See too Lucien Lazare, *Rescue as Resistance: How Jewish Organizations Fought the Holocaust in France,* trans. Jeffrey M. Green (New York: Columbia University Press, 1996), 129.

prisoners of war died in captivity. Although these were soldiers who had military training and were fit for combat, resistance by them was "not notably stronger . . . than that of the Jewish captives in ghettoes or camps." To this should be added Primo Levi's observation that "the gas chambers at Auschwitz were tested on a group of three hundred Russian prisoners of war, young, army-trained, politically indoctrinated, and not hampered by the presence of women and children, and even they did not revolt." Lang concludes that if Holocaust scholars are to ask fairly, "Why didn't *they* resist?" they "must expand its reference beyond the Jews alone."[18]

The phenomenon of Jewish resistance and the diverse forms it assumed are described today not only in specialized monograph studies but even in the most general works on the Holocaust.[19] For one thing, when it was still possible, Jews fled for their safety: well over four hundred thousand German and Austrian Jews left their countries before the outbreak of World War II; over three hundred thousand Polish Jews fled to the Soviet Union; and many others in France and Italy sought refuge in Spain and Switzerland.

Within the ghettos, there were both nonviolent and violent forms of resistance. The nonviolent forms were as simple as smuggling in food, clothing, and medicine, or putting on plays, poetry readings, and art exhibits, creating orchestras, publishing underground newspapers, founding schools, and leaving documentation

18. Berel Lang, "Uncovering Certain Mischievous Questions About the Holocaust," Ina Levine Scholar-in-Residence Annual Lecture (Washington, D.C.: United States Holocaust Memorial Museum, 2002), 5, 6; italics mine. Primo Levi, "Afterword," in *The Reawakening* (New York: Simon & Schuster, 1965), 219.

19. All this information is readily available in the standard histories, dictionaries, and encyclopedias of the Holocaust. I have profited from four such texts: Abraham J. Edelheit and Hershel Edelheit, *History of the Holocaust: A Handbook and Dictionary* (San Francisco: Westview Press, 1994); Jack R. Fischel, *Historical Dictionary of the Holocaust* (Lanham, Md.: Scarecrow Press, 1999); Donald Niewyk and Francis Nicosia, *The Columbia Guide to the Holocaust* (New York: Columbia University Press, 2000); and, above all, the four-volume *Encyclopedia of the Holocaust,* Israel Gutman, editor in chief (New York: Macmillan Publishing Company, 1990).

(writing diaries, for example) of one's experience. All these attempts to remain physically, intellectually, culturally, and morally alive constituted resistance to Nazi restrictions. The three major violent uprisings took place in the Warsaw, Lvov, and Bialystok ghettos. These revolts were undertaken without any hope of forcing the Germans to change their plans regarding Jews. The only hope was that some of the ghetto dwellers might escape to join the partisans. These heroic and futile acts of resistance against insurmountable odds were immediately crushed. There were also armed revolts in several other ghettos, for example, in Cracow, Vilna, and Kovno.

Resistance in the camps also took two forms. Here too, but much more strikingly, any attempt of sick, starving human beings to stay clean, to pray, to read, or to perform any act of maintenance of one's physical, intellectual, or cultural dignity constituted an act of defiance against the systematic dehumanizing process to which they were subjected. There were also Jewish underground resistance groups in many camps, including Maidanek and Buchenwald, and three major armed revolts within the death camps. "In every instance," notes Primo Levi, these armed uprisings "were planned and led by prisoners who were privileged in some way and, consequently, in better physical and spiritual condition than the average camp prisoner."[20] At Treblinka in August 1943, 750 prisoners escaped but only 70 survived the war. At Sobibor in October 1943, 300 prisoners escaped, many of whom were later killed. The Germans liquidated the camp after executing all the remaining prisoners. Finally, in October 1944 in Auschwitz II Birkenau, a group of Jewish *sonderkommandos,* having only explosives for weapons, blew up Crematorium 3 in an effort to stop the extermination of the recently arrived Hungarian Jews. All participants were executed, including the women who provided the explosives. This was an act of pure rebellion with death assured in advance to the participants, an act of heroism performed with the hope of saving lives, of choosing

20. Primo Levi, "Afterword," *The Reawakening,* 217.

to die otherwise than as their captors planned, and of leaving a legacy of resistance. These Jewish-initiated uprisings were the only uprisings against the Nazis in the camps.

In Eastern Europe, Jews escaped from the ghettos to join guerilla outfits struggling against the Germans. In these partisan units, violent Jewish resistance was successful and numerous Jewish participants survived the war. It has been estimated that roughly thirty thousand Jews fought in partisan units in the forests of Belorussia and the western Ukraine alone. Jewish partisan groups also fought with the partisans in Yugoslavia, Bulgaria, and Greece. All of these groups derailed trains, destroyed bridges, and committed various acts of sabotage that took the lives of thousands of Germans. In Western Europe, proportionately speaking, there was a very large percentage of Jews in the underground resistance in France, Italy, and Belgium.

In all of Nazi-occupied Europe, resistance also took the form of rescue, in which Jewish people, particularly Jewish children, were sheltered in non-Jewish institutions, homes, and farms, and were smuggled into non-occupied countries such as Switzerland and Spain. Separating oneself from one's children on the mere hope of their being rescued (and, for reasons of safety, without knowing where one's children would be) was at once the most anguished choice Jewish parents had to make and the ultimate act of resistance against the extermination of European Jewry. Jewish people sometimes played a significant role in the rescue of other Jewish people. In the United States, the American Jewish Committee failed in 1933 in its attempt to get the State Department to protest the treatment of Jews in Germany and, although the American Joint Distribution Committee funded rescue efforts in Europe, American Jews, in the final analysis, were unable to persuade the United States government that the rescue of Jews should be a wartime priority. Jews, however, were soldiers in every army fielded by the Allies. There were over half a million Jews in the United States armed forces during World War II and, among the Allies, Jews constituted by themselves "an army more than 1.5 million strong."[21]

Although it has been relatively neglected among historians until very recently, Jewish resistance in France was also both violent and nonviolent and consisted of armed combat units and an intricate rescue system.[22] The armed struggle of the Jews in France against Vichy and the Nazis took various forms. Although the Jewish population in France in 1940 was less than 1 percent of the general population, a large percentage of primarily French Jews were in the Resistance. They joined early, participated everywhere, and took part in the liberation of Paris. Foreign Jews, less trusting of the government and, generally speaking, the first to resist Vichy actively, tended to join purely Jewish resistance movements, whereas French Jews, many of whom viewed themselves as more French than Jewish, joined various segments of the French Resistance, including the *maquis,* the underground resisters from all levels of society hidden throughout the country in unpopulated areas. Resistance in North Africa was also heavily composed of Jews, and Jews contributed huge sums of money to various resistance operations.

In addition to the Resistance, the non-Communist Jewish *maquis* and Jewish rural fighters referred to as "partisan groups" that also existed throughout the country, the Armée Juive (Jewish Army) played a major role in the armed Jewish resistance in France. Formed in Toulouse in January 1942 by two Zionist activists, Abraham Polonski and Lucien Lublin, it trained Jewish youths to per-

21. *History of the Holocaust,* 107. See too Deborah Dash Moore, *GI/Jews: How World War II Changed a Generation* (Cambridge, Mass.: Harvard University Press, 2004).

22. On Jewish resistance in France, see David Knout, *Contribution à l'histoire de la Résistance juive en France 1940–1944* (Paris: Editions du Centre, 1947); Anny Latour, *La Résistance juive en France (1940–1944);* Lucien Lazare, *Rescue as Resistance: How Jewish Organizations Fought the Holocaust in France.* Also Renée Poznanski, *Les Juifs en France pendant la Seconde Guerre mondiale* (Paris: Hachette, 1994), and Bertram M. Gordan, *Historical Dictionary of World War II France: The Occupation, Vichy, and the Resistance, 1938–1946* (Westport, Conn.: Greenwood Press, 1998).

form military action. At the height of its operations, the Armée Juive had roughly two thousand members. In addition to fighting in the *maquis*, its members set up "hit groups" in major cities such as Paris, Toulouse, Nice, and Lyon to sabotage German installations. They also assassinated collaborators, Gestapo agents, and paid informers on Jews. More than three hundred members of the Armée Juive crossed the Pyrenées to join the five thousand soldiers of the Jewish Brigade of the British Army. Toward the end of the war, the Armée Juive fought at the side of the French Resistance.

In France, as elsewhere, resistance also took the form of rescue, the most successful form of French Jewish resistance. In the Occupied Zone, during the first two years of the Occupation, Jewish groups such as Le Comité de la rue Amelot (Amelot Street Group), Solidarité (Solidarity), and OSE set up soup kitchens, medical dispensaries, and children's services in Paris. After the infamous Vel d'Hiv roundup in July 1942, these groups actually succeeded in getting some children out of the Drancy internment camp. In the south, where tens of thousands of foreign Jews were held in internment camps such as Gurs, Rivesaltes, Récébédou, Le Vernat, Les Milles, and Agde, Jewish social service groups worked in the camps to improve life there materially, culturally, and spiritually. As of 1942, even before the Vel d'Hiv roundup in Paris, the newly set goal was to evacuate the children from the camps.

Once this new plan was initiated, a good deal of illegal activity began. In many cases, for example, guards had to be paid to look the other way. In addition, thousands of false identification papers, false ration cards, false working papers, and false baptismal certificates had to be fabricated. Jewish social workers had to find non-Jewish families and religious institutions willing to shelter these newly liberated children and young adults. Also, hundreds of children with illegal papers were smuggled into Switzerland and Spain.

Two other Jewish groups that played a major role here were Service André (Action Committee Against Deportation) and the Eclai-

reurs Israélites de France (EIF) (French Jewish Scouts). Founded in
1942 in Marseilles by a Russian Jew named Joseph Bass, the Service André worked with Catholic and Protestant groups to fight
the deportation of Jews in Marseilles and the Haute-Loire region
by making false papers and placing children and young adults in
non-Jewish homes in the area. The French Jewish Scouts organization was founded in 1923 by Robert Gamzon. During the Occupation, its members helped in all areas of work: education, social assistance, and rescue. They set up children's homes in the south of
France, sought hideouts for Jewish children of all ages, and with
the help of the Mouvement de jeunesse sioniste (MJS), smuggled
hundreds of young children into Switzerland, and older ones to join
the Jewish Brigade in Spain. In late 1943, the French Jewish Scouts
also created *maquis* units composed in large measure of young Jewish men who had escaped from the internment camps and were ea-
ger to regain their dignity by fighting for the liberation of their people. One hundred fifty French Jewish Scouts died in battle during
the Occupation.

Very little rescue work would have succeeded, however, without
the incredible generosity of the American Joint Distribution Committee. A Jewish foundation created in 1914 to help Jews threatened with famine in Palestine, it now spent millions of dollars to
help pay for food, medicine, the housing of thousands of children
in hiding, and the *passeurs* (smugglers) who led so many of them
into Switzerland. No rescue work could have succeeded without the
help of so many non-Jewish organizations—such as the American
Friends Service Committee, the YMCA, the Unitarian Service Committee, the Red Cross, Amitié Chrétienne (Christian Friendship),
the very important Protestant women's relief organization La Cimade—and the countless thousands of French men and women,
secular and religious, who took thousands of Jewish children into
their homes and religious institutions. Approximately eleven thousand Jewish children living in France were deported during the Oc-

cupation. It is now estimated that in France somewhere between ten thousand and twenty thousand Jewish children were either hidden or smuggled out of the country. It is therefore probable that at least twice as many children would have been deported without this rescue work.

OSE was the principal Jewish organization concerned with the welfare of foreign Jews in the internment camps in the south of France, the ultimate evacuation of Jewish children from those camps, and the placing of those children in non-Jewish homes and institutions.[23] Founded in Russia in 1912 by a group of young doctors committed to offering poor Jews sanitary protection and health benefits, this medical-social welfare organization moved in 1917 and later opened offices in Poland in 1922, and in Berlin in 1923, where its first president was Albert Einstein. In 1933, when it had over thirteen thousand members in ten countries, OSE moved to Paris. In 1940, its main office was moved to Vichy, then to Montpellier. In early 1942, it had 280 official employees.

In November 1941, when Vivette Samuel arrived in Rivesaltes, there were over twenty-eight thousand foreign Jews held in internment camps in the south of France. Roughly five thousand of these internees were children under the age of eighteen. Jewish social workers from OSE, such as Vivette Samuel, hoped to help feed, clothe, and bolster the morale of these detainees. The conditions in the camps were atrocious. With help from such non-Jewish organizations as the Quakers, the Red Cross, La Cimade, Secours Suisse, the YMCA, and the Unitarian Service Committee, social work-

23. On the question of rescue and OSE in particular, in addition to the books listed in the previous footnote, see Vivette Samuel, *Sauver les enfants* (Paris: Liana Levi, 1995); Martine Lemalet, ed., *Au secours des enfants du siècle. Regards croisés sur l'O.S.E.* (Paris: Nil Editions, 1993); Sabine Zeitoun, *L'Oeuvre de Secours aux Enfants (O.S.E.) sous l'Occupation en France* (Paris: L'Harmattan, 1990); Sabine Zeitoun, *Ces Enfants qu'il fallait sauver* (Paris: Albin Michel, 1989); Hillel J. Kieval, "Legality and Resistance in Vichy France: The Rescue of Jewish Children," *Proceedings of the American Philosophical Society* 124 (October 1980): 339–66.

ers raised the daily caloric intake from five hundred to a thousand, expanded the distribution of medicines, organized a theater, established a library, and celebrated Jewish holidays. Nevertheless, conditions remained lamentable in every way.

It soon became obvious that the primary goal of OSE had to be to evacuate the children from the camps. Thanks in large measure to the constant pleas of Dr. Joseph Weill, an Alsatian physician affiliated with OSE, almost all the children had been evacuated from the camps before August 2, 1942, the date of the first transfer of Jewish refugees from the camps in the south of France to Drancy and then to the death camps in Poland. Vivette Samuel played a major role in convincing Jewish women to give up their children. At first, it was legal to take children out of the camps if they were under fifteen years of age and had a certificate of lodging signed by the prefect of the appropriate geographical region. When that became illegal—because the Vichy government (not the Germans) decided that Jewish children would also be deported—OSE began to operate illegally as well as legally. Andrée Salomon, a tremendously important OSE worker in the camps, and others among her equally devoted co-workers, lied about the ages of the children, disguised them for purposes of evacuation, paid off guards, fabricated false exit passes, and did everything else required to get the children out of the camps.

Once they were outside the camps, there were several options for placing the thousands of children involved. Thanks to funding from the American Joint Distribution Committee, in July 1941, OSE established eight homes for children in the Unoccupied Zone. These homes, as well as others created shortly thereafter, housed hundreds of mostly foreign Jewish children and adolescents. Here, as Lisa Gossels depicts in her outstanding 2000 documentary *The Children of Chabannes*, OSE workers, such as Rachel Pludermacher and Georges Loinger in the château of Chabannes that sheltered four hundred Jewish refugees, tried to give these children, most of whom would never see their parents again, as normal a life as possible. They pragmatically insisted that the children stay in excellent physical shape. They organized cultural, spiritual, and educational activities including dances, plays, and orchestra work. Eventually, it became too dangerous to keep all these Jewish children together. The homes were then dismantled and the children dispersed for their own safety. That it was prudent to disassemble these homes was tragically confirmed by what happened on April 6, 1944, at Izieu, in a home that was then being dismantled. Led by Klaus Barbie, a Gestapo raid captured forty-four children and the staff. Only one staff member returned from the camps. "In all," notes Chana Arnon, "during the war 32 OSE staff members lost their lives, and approximately 90 OSE children did not survive."[24]

Once the option of the OSE homes was no longer viable, the other two options became even more crucial. The first, the placing of children in non-Jewish families and religious institutions, had always been operational but now increased significantly. Once again, many non-Jewish organizations such as the Quakers, the Red Cross, the YMCA, and the Unitarians were essential in this endeavor. The second option, smuggling children into Switzerland, was extremely dangerous. Consequently, it was limited while children were relatively safe in the Unoccupied Zone. As of August 1942, however, when Jewish men, women, and children were rounded up also in the Unoccupied Zone, and particularly as of November 1942, when there was no longer an Unoccupied Zone, smuggling children became a good alternative. Between May 1943 and June 1944, more than fifteen hundred children and adolescents were smuggled into Switzerland by OSE, EIF, and MJS. Here again, non-Jewish groups, particularly La Cimade, were indispensable, but OSE itself had Georges Loinger, who shepherded hundreds of children into Switzerland.

24. Chana Arnon, "Introduction: Jews Rescued Jews during the Holocaust," 2. Manuscript in my possession.

The illegal work of OSE began spontaneously, dramatically, and ecumenically on August 29, 1942, the famous *"nuit de Vénissieux"* (Vénissieux Night). Twelve hundred Jews, including roughly a hundred children, had been rounded up on August 26 in the Unoccupied Zone and held near Lyon at a camp in Vénissieux. OSE workers, Dr. Joseph Weill and Charles Lederman; Father Glasberg, Jewish by birth; Father Chaillet; and members of Amitié Chrétienne (a Catholic/Protestant group united in the struggle against anti-Semitism) had received orders that the children were to be deported to Drancy along with the adults. They kept the orders secret, gathered the children, put them under the charge of Cardinal Gerlier, archbishop of Lyon, and refused to hand over the children or to give the address where they were being held. With this sudden, deceptive act, over one hundred children were saved from deportation and OSE had gone underground with its Christian allies.

Just after this bold undertaking, Joseph Weill asked Charles Lederman's brother-in-law, Georges Garel, a thirty-three-year-old engineer of Russian origin who had witnessed *la nuit de Vénissieux* but had never been involved in Jewish rescue, if he would be willing, since he was completely unknown to the authorities, to organize a rescue network for children. Garel gave up his job in the Resistance and, in the aftermath of *la nuit de Vénissieux,* the *circuit Garel* (Garel Network) was born. It constituted the first entirely clandestine network for rescuing Jewish children in the still-unoccupied zone.

Thus Catholic, Protestant, Jewish, and secular forces joined together to shelter Jewish children in individual non-Jewish families and institutions, furnishing them with false papers, false ration cards, and all they needed for survival. Garel got help, not only from Gerlier and Amitié Chrétienne, but also from Monsignor Saliège, archbishop of Toulouse; Monsignor Théas, bishop of Montauban; La Cimade; and other Protestant groups and individual pastors in Protestant villages, and various independent people. In less than a year, from late August 1942 onward, the Garel Network, with headquarters in Lyon and Garel in charge of all operations, placed over sixteen hundred Jewish children in various parts of France. Sabine Zeitoun estimates that of the more than five thousand children saved by OSE, the Garel Network saved three thousand of them.[25] It was a group of roughly three dozen, mostly female, mostly Jewish, mostly OSE employees who, like Madeleine Dreyfus, working independently and, generally speaking, unknown to one another, took these children on the very dangerous train or bus rides from Lyon to the homes or farms where they were hidden.

When we consider, on the one hand, all this nonviolent resistance as well as the violent resistance that Jews took part in throughout Europe during the Holocaust and, on the other, the hopelessness of the situation in most quarters (the lack of arms, of training, of a home country, the general indifference of non-Jews) and the vicious reprisals taken by the Nazis, it is less surprising that not all Jews resisted than it is that so many did in so many different ways. It is thus unconscionable to continue to speak in general terms of "Jewish passivity." Doing so violates the historical record and plays into the hands of anti-Semites who claim that Jews brought their misfortunes upon themselves.[26]

25. Sabine Zeitoun, L'Oeuvre de Secours aux Enfants, 193.
26. It is encouraging that historians are spending more time on resistance. The new five-volume Auschwitz 1940–1945, for example, contains four hundred pages on camp resistance movements at Auschwitz. Another very good sign is that playwrights (e.g., Brian Silberman in his Manifest) and novelists—Ian MacMillan, Village of a Million Spirits (Steerforth Press, 1999), and Rich Cohen, The Avengers (Alfred Knopf, 2000)—are writing about specific instances of Jewish resistance. Finally, the U.S. Holocaust Memorial Museum has announced the Miles Lerman Center for the Study of Jewish Resistance Research Fellowship and Yad Vashem has announced a project to establish a Chair in the Rescue of Jews by Jews at their Institute for Holocaust Research.

⌒

I maintained lasting friendships in Le Chambon and for all its inhabitants a sense of gratitude that will live as long as I do.

Madeleine Dreyfus

She was a woman of conscience with a strong social sense.

Lili-Elise Garel

After eighteen months of prison and concentration camp incarceration, Madeleine was repatriated on May 18, 1945. In a two-page untitled typescript found among her papers, she portrays the late but magnificent arrival of spring 1945:

Spring 1945, still trapped behind these sinister barbed wires, under surveillance day and night, by these implacable watchtowers, punished, scorned, dying of hunger, of vermin, surrounded, gripped more and more tightly by an approaching Death. . . . It wasn't Spring . . . Spring 1945. Interminable fifteen day voyage, dying of hunger, of typhus, of dysentery, living on nettles, dandelions, beets. . . . And then . . . Spring 1945, we finally found you, we finally met you on our way. . . . Spring 1945, it was finally these three unforgettable hours when, as on a magic carpet, we were miraculously transported to France. It was this Marseillaise that first welcomed us and these arms of our compatriots that embraced us. Spring, you were not an illusion; we had finally found you.

Madeleine landed in Le Bourget and went first to the Hôtel Lutetia to fulfill the necessary formalities and then, on the *métro,* as if "this entire life of nightmares had never existed," to her friend Suzanne Tourneur's to spend her first night back in France. The next day, "this miraculous Saturday," as her husband would still call it over forty years later, she met Raymond, found the husbands of Madeleine Lang and Marcelle Christophe to give them the address where their wives were being held in the Russian zone in Saxony, and took the train with Raymond to Lyon where their children were waiting. That there would be a good deal of catching up to do could be seen when Raymond asked twenty-one-month-old Annette to give her mother a kiss and Annette "rushed toward the fireplace in her bedroom and kissed the photograph of Madeleine, the photograph that she had had for so long before her eyes."

In 1946, Madeleine worked again for OSE with its "medical-pedagogical team" in Paris. OSE workers still had hundreds of children on their hands and in their hearts, children whose parents had not returned from the camps and who had not been claimed by other family members. Madeleine counseled many of these children and others, referred to as "the children of Buchenwald," with severe re-adaptation problems. In 1947, she received "the Resistance medal."

Madeleine soon left OSE, however, to develop her career, in private practice but above all with the Institut de formation et d'études psychosociologiques et pédagogiques (IFEPP), which she helped found and from which she retired in 1974. In 1957, she participated in the first Group Psychotherapy Conference in Zurich. She translated from English into French many texts dealing with Adlerian psychology. She was also a counselor near Paris at the Institution Sainte Geneviève d'Asnières and a frequent lecturer and workshop organizer in schools throughout the Paris area. She remained in close touch with well-known Adlerians, such as Sophie Lazarsfeld (whom she often visited in New York) and Manès Sperber, finding renewed inspiration in them for her own participation in workshops throughout the world. In all of her professional encounters, Madeleine distinguished herself as an Adlerian psychologist and psychotherapist particularly gifted as a teacher in dealing with children and family situations.

In many ways, however, Madeleine never left OSE or Le Chambon-sur-Lignon. She concludes her "Extraits d'un témoignage," for example, a December 1983, eleven-page typescript in which she outlines her work with OSE from October 1941 until shortly after the end of the war, by noting: "That's where my OSE career stops, but not the friendly contact that existed among all of us 'survivors': Boëgie, Germaine Masour, Vivette and Julien Samuel . . . friends that I still have! Georges Garel, Julien, Germaine have left us, but will always be with us." The same can be said about her friends in Le Chambon-sur-Lignon—Madame Lebrat, Madame Déléage, Marcel Déléage, Eva Phillit, to name only the most important ones—whom she and her family visited often from the liberation onward. In addition, in June 1979, Madeleine and Raymond attended the ceremony at which the plaque expressing the gratitude of the Jewish refugees hidden "on this land of refuge" was dedicated and placed across from the Protestant church in Le Chambon-sur-Lignon. They were also present at the Israeli Embassy in Paris in 1982 when Magda Trocmé received the Righteous Gentile medal from Yad Vashem. Madeleine Dreyfus died on January 10, 1987, and is buried in the family vault in the Cimetière Montmartre. Reflecting on her last years, her son Michel writes: "The last years of her life were marked, it seemed to me, by a certain inner peace, although in my opinion, her original frustration never left her."[27]

Many years after her liberation from the camps, Michel Dreyfus asked his mother how she decided to get involved in rescue activity. She told him "that she never had the sense of really making a choice, that events had taken place in such a way that she found herself in a dangerous situation without having been fully aware of it."[28] Perhaps the best answer to this question, in Adlerian terms, is that Madeleine's lifetime behavioral pattern (her "lifestyle"), from her youth onward, was one of service to others. The fact that rendering that service in Lyon in 1942 became a matter of life and death did not seem to matter. What mattered was what always mattered to her before her arrest, in the camps, and after her liberation: concern for others. The circumstances in her life changed

27. Letter from Michel Dreyfus to author, October 23, 1999.
28. Ibid.

but she always exhibited the same qualities of friendship, under-standing, sympathy, and solidarity. Raymond considered the word "*écoute*" ("listen"), the title of his biographical memoir of Madeleine, "the key-word of her action":

> This word "*écoute*" sums up in my view what Madeleine was during her lifetime, at the family level, obviously, but how much more so still at the professional level; because she always had an attentive ear for her interlocutors, of all ages, of both sexes; she always tried to bring to those who came to her the response they were waiting for, or at least she tried to understand and help them in their quest for the solution they needed. . . . That's what she wanted all her life.

If we do not count as rescuers Jewish parents who saved their children by sending them into hiding or into a neutral country, then there is one common trait that unites all rescuers of Jews during the Holocaust: their "universe of obligation" transcended their im-mediate families. Psychiatrist Eva Fogelman writes about the trau-ma that this often caused the children of rescuers: "Many children of rescuers felt abandoned. The lives of rescuers and of their fami-lies were in disarray; rescuers were put in jeopardy in order to help people who were not related to them in any way."[29] Although he felt that his children "were learning the lessons of life quite young," An-dré Trocmé asks, regarding the constant flow into his home of peo-ple to be rescued: "In this whirlwind, what becomes of our family life?" His response: "We are so rarely alone with our children. We suffer because of it; so do they."[30] Concerning the Dreyfus family, in addition to his insistence that Madeleine cease her clandestine work after Annette's birth in August 1943, Raymond remarks that "Annette experienced difficulties in early adolescence, undoubt-edly due to the fact that she had been abruptly taken away from

29. Eva Fogelman, *Conscience and Courage: The Rescuers of Jews During the Holo-caust* (New York: Doubleday, 1994), 305.
30. Magda Trocmé, "Souvenirs Autobiographiques," "Lettre d'André à Simone," 248.

her mother in early infancy." Annette herself refers to her mother's "frequent absences" and the fact that "my mother, during her entire life, was always between two meetings." For his part, Michel writes: "If she was not always a very gifted mother—do such mothers exist?—she was a very good psychologist and her success in that domain demonstrates it."[31] In the same letter, he notes that when he reproached his mother "for having taken so many risks when she was the mother of three children, one of whom was a three-month-old daughter, she seemed to ask herself the question for the first time, without finding an answer."

Most children of rescuers, Fogelman concludes, ultimately come to accept their parents' decisions. The same is true in this case. Michel refers to his mother as "a veritable heroine" who stood up to Klaus Barbie, helped her fellow camp inmates, and never lost her dignity. Annette, who claims to take after her mother in that she as well is not "a housewife," points out that, despite her professional commitments, Madeleine "succeeded in 'concentrating' her presence in her family . . . I admired her. I loved her." Like her mother, Annette too exhibits great concern for others, having founded an association, AMILA ("A Friend Is There"), for persons with psychiatric problems. Nonetheless, as Fogelman concludes, it is absolutely essential to recognize publicly the risks and sacrifices made by the rescuers: "Public honors and recognition of their parents as moral exemplars have helped soothe the anger and hurt. Such recognition has given the children of rescuers the comfort of knowing that their parents' sacrifice and their own suffering made a difference."[32]

In his comprehensive and stimulating study *Saving The Jews: Amazing Stories of Men and Women Who Defied the "Final Solution,"* Mordecai Paldiel explains: "At Yad Vashem, the purpose of the Righteous program was and remains to single out persons who, irrespective of their private opinions and inclinations, stood morally firm

31. Letter from Michel Dreyfus to author, October 23, 1999.
32. Eva Fogelman, *Conscience and Courage*, 305.

when faced with the challenge presented by the Holocaust. By saving Jews, in spite of the tremendous risks to themselves, they sustained the image of man as a moral, caring and compassionate being."[33] Paldiel then remarks correctly that these acts of rescue concretize the moral philosophy of Emmanuel Levinas, who holds that "true ethics begins with turning towards and responding to the other, leading to a commitment to caring for the other person's needs."[34]

So far so good. But when Paldiel goes on to justify the exclusion of Jews from the title of "Righteous Among the Nations," he violates both his earlier statement that people were chosen "irrespective of their private opinions and inclinations" and the spirit of Levinas, who stood for infinite responsibility to the absolutely other and would not have seen any such dichotomy between Jews and non-Jews. Here is how Paldiel draws his distinction: "The title of 'Righteous Among the Nations' is, of course, reserved for non-Jews who risked their lives to save Jews from the Nazis and their collaborators during the Holocaust. The logic behind it resides in the theory that whereas Jews who saved their brethren Jews only fulfilled their obligation, non-Jews had no such responsibility toward their Jewish neighbors; hence, those that braved the risks to themselves by extending help to Jews merit a special distinction."[35]

Some specific texts in the Hebrew Bible and the Christian Apostolic Writings, however, show that this distinction fails. Both Christians and Jews have an obligation toward all children of Adam. One of the key passages is Leviticus 19:18: "You shall not take vengeance or bear a grudge against any of your people, but you shall love your neighbor as yourself." Rabbi Akiba comments, "This is a great principle in the Torah."[36] Precisely what it means, however, has been

33. Mordecai Paldiel, *Saving the Jews: Amazing Stories of Men and Women Who Defied the "Final Solution"* (Rockville, Md.: Schreiber Publishing, 2000), 267.

34. Ibid.   35. Ibid., 272.

36. Hayim Nahman Bialik and Yehoshua Hana Ravnitzky, eds., *The Book of Legends: Legends From the Talmud and Midrash* (New York: Schocken Books, 1992), 646 (paragraph 48).

less easily ascertained. Although "neighbor" here is more often read as "fellow Israelite," this has not always been the case. Ben Azzai's commentary on this verse, for example, is the following: "This is the book of the descendants of Adam . . . him whom God made in his likeness."[37] In this reading, "neighbor" means every descendant of Adam, all of whom have been made in God's likeness. Whatever the meaning of the word "neighbor" here and elsewhere in the Hebrew Bible, however, Leviticus 19:34 shows that the commandment to love transcends the covenant community: "The alien who resides with you shall be to you as the citizen among you; you shall love the alien as yourself, for you were aliens in the land of Egypt. . . ."

In the Christian Apostolic Writings, when Jesus is asked to name the greatest commandments (Matthew 22:34–40; Mark 12:28–34) or what one must do to inherit eternal life (Luke 10:25–28), he cites two specific passages from the Hebrew Bible (Deuteronomy 6:5; Leviticus 19:18): "You shall love the Lord your God with all your heart, and with all your soul, and with all your strength, and with all your mind; and your neighbor as yourself" (Luke 10:27). Then, in Luke's account, perhaps to draw Jesus into a debate going on within Judaism at the time, a lawyer asks him: "And who is my neighbor?" (Luke 10:29) Jesus responds to this inquiry by narrating the parable of the Good Samaritan (Luke 10:30–37), in which a Jew is beaten by robbers and left half dead by the roadside. Neither a priest nor a Levite who passed by stopped to help him. But a Samaritan, a foreigner not expected to show sympathy to Jews, bandaged his wounds, took him to an inn and paid for his keep. "Which of these three," Jesus asks, "do you think was a neighbor to the man who fell into the hands of the robbers?" The lawyer answers: "The one who showed him mercy," to which Jesus responds: "Go and do likewise."

37. Ibid., 643 (paragraph 21). For a discussion of the word "neighbor" in the Hebrew Bible and the New Testament, see *The Oxford Companion to the Bible*, ed. Bruce M. Metzger and Michael D. Coogan (New York: Oxford University Press, 1993), 555–56.

There can be no doubt regarding Christ's teaching here where He speaks out explicitly against religious exclusivity, defining our neighbor as anyone in need regardless of ethnic or religious origin. The whole series of formal public apologies by national Christian churches and by the Vatican have taken place, not because Christians have no obligations toward Jews, but precisely because Christians have recognized that they did not fulfill those obligations to Jews during the Holocaust.

The status of Jewish rescuers of Jews appears even more bizarre as of 2004, when Yad Vashem, for the first time to its knowledge, recognized two men born Jewish, Father Alexandre Glasberg and his brother Vila, as "Righteous Among the Nations." These men were not posthumously recognized as Jews but as "Righteous Gentiles" and they could not have been more deserving. Nonetheless, we now have a strange situation in which Christians who rescued Jews and persons born Jewish who converted to Christianity and rescued Jews have been publicly recognized for their courageous deeds, but Jewish people who rescued Jews have never been so recognized.

To insist on these differences violates the spirit of the overwhelming majority of rescuers, both Jews and Christians alike, who did not think in terms of religious differences when they performed their courageous deeds. Throughout her life, Madeleine Dreyfus upheld this expansive "universe of obligation" and identified with a common humanity. Consider Raymond's account of her experiences in the Vexin, where she taught for a year. This was "a village populated with farmworkers, modern slaves, living in extreme poverty, lodged in hovels that resembled pigsties." Here is how she understood a fundamental human condition for which we are all responsible: "Madeleine confided to me the sense of shame she felt in the presence of these children who had been forgotten by Progress and the Republic." Furthermore, she underscored the fact that the ethical commandments of the Hebrew Bible bind all Christians and

Jews alike. She writes about the people of Le Chambon-sur-Lignon: "they had come to the aid of their neighbors, as the Old Testament said, the Bible of the Jews and of Christians." It was, therefore, Raymond claims, "completely natural for me to turn toward them in the distress I found myself in, this time for the protection of my own children." Had the situation been different, he and Madeleine would have felt the same moral obligation the non-Jewish rescuers did. In all I have read by and about her, there is not a single word that would indicate that her reasons for rescuing potential victims of the Nazis were any different from those of the majority of other rescuers. Madeleine did not risk her life to save these children because they were Jewish. She did so because they were children.

This was also true in the case of Félix Chevrier and Janusz Korczak. In Lisa Gossel's award-winning documentary *The Children of Chabannes,* Félix Chevrier, the Gentile leader of a rescue mission that sheltered four hundred Jewish children in an OSE home in Chabannes, is described as having been anguished throughout the entire rescue period "because he didn't want to save the children because they were Jewish. He wanted to save them because they were children." The great Jewish humanitarian, pediatrician, and teacher, Janusz Korczak, who ran an orphanage in the Warsaw Ghetto, when asked what he would do after the war, as related in Andrzej Wajda's 1990 film entitled *Korczak,* responded: "Take care of German orphans."

We defile the memory of the rescuers, Jews and Christians alike, when we confine them to categories that their magnanimous souls obviously transcended. Although there were Christians, such as Mme Brottes, who appears in *Weapons of the Spirit,* for whom it was essential that they were rescuing Jews ("God's people"),[38] and

---

38. This is important too in the account given by Lawrence Baron: "Parochialism, Patriotism, and Philo-Semitism: Why Members of the Reformed Churches Rescued Jews in the Netherlands during the Holocaust," paper presented at the 28th annual Scholars' Conference on the Holocaust and the Churches (Seattle, 1998).

Jews, as Ken Waltzer's important work on the Jewish underground in Poland has shown, who were rescuing Jews ("the remnants of a nation") because they were Jews,[39] for the great majority of rescuers, the "Jewishness" of the person to be rescued was not an issue. By their own admission, this majority was affirming the fundamental similarity among all human beings. All those, Madeleine Dreyfus among them, who performed these exemplary deeds of rescue have earned the name "Righteous," a term that should be conferred for having *done* something, not for *being,* or not being, a member of a particular religion. Prudence dictated that both Christians and Jews lie low, out of risk's path. All those who chose to rise up in the name of others deserve recognition. Yad Vashem should not create a category called "Righteous Jews." Much more fittingly, there should be only one category, "The Righteous," or, perhaps, "The Rescuers," to which would belong all persons who risked their lives to rescue Jews during the Holocaust.

39. Kenneth Waltzer, "Jewish Underground and the Rescue of Jews in Poland," paper presented at the 35th annual Scholars' Conference on the Holocaust and the Churches (Philadelphia, March 8, 2005).

4

Albert Camus' *The Plague*

Up to this point, we have dealt with the people who rescued Jews on the plateau during the Holocaust. The future Nobel Prize winner Albert Camus also lived on the plateau at this time. He was simply a visitor who had a completely different connection to the area. He was not part of any network and did not rescue Jews. But as a writer attentive to what was going on around him, he incorporated local people and events into the novel he was writing, which portrayed, in allegorical form, the conditions of life in Occupied France. He published that widely acclaimed novel, *The Plague*, in 1947.

Although Camus had conceived the novel in Algeria as early as 1941, he wrote it in France. The writing itself was extremely onerous and, along with *The Rebel*, *The Plague* was the most difficult of his works to bring to fruition. As he struggled to write it, he came to doubt his ability as a writer and denigrated his text in his *Notebooks*. But *The Plague*, this burden that weighed upon him for so long, more than any other of his works accounted for his being awarded the Noble Prize in Literature in 1957. For fourteen or fifteen months, Camus worked intensely on the novel while living in a small hamlet near Le Chambon-sur-Lignon, where both violent and nonviolent resistance to Nazism and the Vichy regime was taking place. He was fully aware of the violent and nonviolent resistance going on around him and he subtly incorporated it into his narrative.

In July 1942, Albert Camus' Polish doctor and friend, Stanislas Cviklinski, advised him to leave Algiers and spend the winter in the mountains in France. Since January of that year, both of his lungs had been infected with tuberculosis and he was in a weakened state. Before the end of August, Camus and his wife, Francine, were settled in Panelier,[1] a hamlet belonging to the commune of Le Mazet-Saint-Voy, situated about two miles from Le Chambon-sur-Lignon at an elevation just under three thousand feet in the Massif Central on the plateau Vivarais-Lignon. The choice of Panelier was simple. Francine's aunt, Marguerite Faure, had married the actor Paul Oettly, whose mother, Sarah, ran a boarding house there. During their childhood, Francine and her sisters spent their vacations at the boarding house.

In October, Francine went back to Oran, their home in Algeria, to her teaching position. Albert remained on the plateau to continue taking treatments for his lungs. Yet from what his friend Pascal Pia writes to him on September 15, 1942—"You tell me it is highly unlikely you will spend the winter in Panelier"[2]—Camus did not expect to spend much more time there. A few weeks after this letter from Pia, Camus had Pia book passage for him on a steamer to Algeria. But the Allies invaded North Africa on the night of November 7 and four days later the Germans headed south to occupy the

1. All of Camus' critics and biographers refer to "Le Panelier," but I follow the people in Le Chambon-sur-Lignon who call it "Panelier." The information regarding Camus' Polish doctor and friend is in Olivier Todd, *Albert Camus, une vie* (Paris: Gallimard, 1996), 301.
2. Albert Camus and Pascal Pia, *Correspondance 1939–1947*, ed. Yves Marc Ajchenbaum (Paris: Fayard/Gallimard, 2000), Letter from Pia (15 September 1942), 104. See too Gérard Bollon, *Les séjours d'Albert Camus sur le plateau Vellave (1942–1952)* (Saint-Jeures: L'Atelier du Moulin, 2006), 16. Most commentators establish Camus' sojourn on the plateau from late August 1942 to November 1943. Bollon, alone to my knowledge, limits Camus' stay to fourteen months, "from August 20, 1942 to October 19, 1943" (p. 10).

Postcard of Panelier, the hamlet where Albert Camus lived and worked on *The Plague* from August 1942 until late 1943. *Courtesy of Gérard Bollon and Annik Flaud.*

formerly Vichy-controlled zone of France. As the November 11 entry in his *Notebooks* indicates: "November 11th. Like rats!"[3] Camus was trapped.

He ultimately remained on the plateau in Panelier until late 1943. With the monthly checks for twenty-five hundred francs that he began to receive from his publisher, Gallimard, in December 1942, he could easily get by. Every twelve days he had to make the roughly thirty-five-mile trip from Panelier to Saint-Etienne for his pneumothorax injections. Not only were these trips more and more difficult as winter set in, but, as Camus says in his *Notebooks*, this dreary industrial city depressed him no end: "Saint-Etienne and its

3. Albert Camus, *Carnets*, January 1942–March 1951 (Paris: Gallimard, 1964), 53. In further references to this volume of Camus' *Carnets*, page numbers are inserted parenthetically in the text.

suburbs. Such a sight is the condemnation of the civilization that brought it into being. A world where there is no longer any place for living, for joy, for active leisure, is a world that ought to die. No people can live without beauty" (92). At the same time, his letters to Pia, to whom he dedicated *The Myth of Sisyphus,* uniformly depict his alienation and loneliness: "my country of wind and cold . . . I once again have the impression of being in the middle of nowhere"; "the country is very sad and lonely"; "here I lead the same solitary and silent life."[4] It is no wonder that, like many Jews also trapped in the south of France, Camus thought about escaping to Algeria through Spain.[5] In mid-October or early November 1943, he moved permanently to Paris, fleeing the solitude of Panelier for work at Gallimard as a "secretary-reader." With *The Stranger* in print and *The Myth of Sisyphus* ready to see the light of day (without the chapter on Kafka, which was removed by the German censor), he was the clandestine figure "Albert Mathé, born in Choisy-le-Roi and living in Epinay-sur-Orge" and the coeditor with Pia of *Combat,* a Resistance newspaper that sold 180,000 copies a day in Occupied France.[6]

While on the plateau during the war, Camus was in touch not only with Pascal Pia, whom he had known since 1938. He also met the Catholic resistance poet René Leynaud, who was arrested in Lyon in May 1944 and shot to death in the woods outside Villeneuve a few weeks later. Leynaud was deeply involved in Resistance activity in Lyon, where Camus spent time with him and Pia. Camus was particularly fond of Leynaud, to whom he dedicated his *Letters to a German Friend.* He also wrote a preface to the posthumous edition of his poetry, in which he speaks mostly of their friendship and the time they spent together in Lyon and Saint-Etienne in 1943. Camus saw Leynaud for the last time in Paris in the spring of 1944:

4. Camus and Pia, *Correspondance,* Letters from Camus (11 December 1942; 29 December 1942; 28 January 1943), 120; 128; 132.
5. Ibid., 123n.
6. Ibid., xxi; xxii.

"In thirty years of life," he notes, "never has the death of a man had such an impact on me."[7]

Camus introduced Leynaud to another Christian friend, the anti-Fascist Nietzschean Dominican priest Father Raymond-Léopold Brückberger, whom he met through Michel Gallimard. Camus refers to Brückberger as "an energetic and rebellious Dominican, who claimed to detest Christian democrats and dreamed of a Nietzschean Christianity."[8] Through Pia, Camus also met Francis Ponge, with whom he had a long correspondence. Ponge had on occasion stayed at Panelier and had married a woman from Le Chambon-sur-Lignon.[9] Camus was intrigued by Ponge's collection of prose poems, *Le Parti pris des choses,* which later had a profound, if temporary, influence on the post-World War II novel.

Herbert Lottman maintains that Camus knew hardly anyone on the plateau: "Outsider that he was, Camus didn't know these good people and they had little opportunity to get to know him."[10] Camus' biographers, however, have all been to some degree deficient in interviewing important people there. None of the three major biographers (Lottman, Patrick McCarthy, and Olivier Todd),[11] for example, quote Oscar Rosowsky who, while hiding on the plateau during the Occupation, forged several thousand false identity papers. In one of his writings about his clandestine work, "Les faux papiers d'identité au Chambon-sur-Lignon 1942–1944," Rosowsky refers to a certain farmer named Jean Bouix from the commune Le Mazet-Saint-Voy who spent time searching for Jews without false papers, trying to convince them to obtain them. Rosowsky refers to Bouix

7. Albert Camus, "Introduction aux 'Poésies Posthumes' de René Leynaud," in *Essais* (Paris: Gallimard, Bibliothèque de la Pléiade, 1965), 1477.

8. Ibid., 1476.

9. Herbert R. Lottman, *Albert Camus: A Biography* (Garden City, N.Y.: Doubleday, 1979), 259.

10. Ibid., 273.

11. In addition to Lottman, I am referring to Patrick McCarthy, *Camus: A Critical Study of his Life and Work* (London: Hamish Hamilton, 1982), and to Camus' most gifted biographer, Olivier Todd, whose *Albert Camus, une vie* is definitive.

as a "friend of Albert Camus."[12] Bouix's name does not appear in any biography of Albert Camus.

Of the three major biographers, only Todd interviewed Pierre Fayol. This was an enormous mistake on the part of Lottman and McCarthy. Had Lottman, for example, interviewed Fayol (né Lévy), one of the top Resistance leaders in the area of Le Chambon-sur-Lignon, he never would have written that "resistance activity was taking place in Le Chambon-sur-Lignon of which Camus was not aware, or was only partially aware, perhaps because of the impermanence of his association with the region."[13] Fayol, who visited and even stayed on occasion in Panelier for reasons of safety, speaks often of Camus in his writings. In his "Formes de Résistance armée sur le Plateau," he mentions his "frequent meetings with Albert Camus" and the fact that Camus introduced him to Brückberger and Ponge.[14] Elsewhere he points out that Camus gave him one of the first issues of the periodical *Les Etoiles* (later to appear as *Les Lettres françaises*), which contained patriotic poems by Aragon and Eluard that he copied for members of the Resistance. He notes too that Camus gave him the manuscripts of *Caligula* and *The Misunderstanding* and that "our relationship became a very friendly one."[15] In a July 1994 interview, Fayol's wife, Marianne, insists that, although Camus was sick and under treatment for his tuberculosis, "he was light-hearted and full of energy. We went swimming together. He was a very interesting and pleasant friend."[16]

On the other hand, only Lottman interviewed André Chouraqui, Camus' Jewish friend from Algeria, who replaced Madeleine

12. Dr. Oscar Rosowsky, "Les faux papiers d'identité au Chambon-sur-Lignon 1942–1944," in Bolle et al., *Le Plateau Vivarais-Lignon*, 243. See also page 306 of the same volume.

13. Lottman, *Albert Camus: A Biography*, 272.

14. Pierre Fayol, "Formes de Résistance armée sur le Plateau," in Bolle et al., *Le Plateau Vivarais-Lignon*, 467.

15. Pierre Fayol, *Le Chambon-sur-Lignon sous l'occupation*, 156–57.

16. Unpublished interview with Barbara Barnett (July 1994). A copy of this interview is in my possession.

Postcard of Tence, a village where Camus often visited his friend André Chouraqui, with whom he discussed the significance of the plague in the Hebrew Bible. *Courtesy of Annik Flaud.*

Dreyfus after her arrest and worked clandestinely for OSE, taking Jewish children to the plateau for shelter. The future assistant mayor of Jerusalem and author of an influential autobiography, *L'Amour fort comme la mort,* also did other very dangerous resistance work seeking shelter for activists and political refugees.[17] An important biblical scholar who later translated the Hebrew Bible into French, Chouraqui helped Camus decipher the significance of the plague in the Bible as he worked on his novel in Panelier,[18] and invited him to his hideout in Chaumargeais, a hamlet in the nearby commune of

17. Chouraqui relates his experiences on the plateau during World War II in his autobiography, *L'Amour fort comme la mort* (Paris: Editions Robert Laffont, 1990), 232–42.

18. Lottman, *Albert Camus: A Biography,* 273.

Tence, where they talked at length about their situation while eating Algerian food.[19]

Camus must have known many other people living on the plateau. Despite Philip Hallie's claim, "I heard that Camus had met, at least once, the leader of the village, Pastor André Trocmé . . . ,"[20] I cannot establish that Camus ever met either of the Protestant pastors André Trocmé or Edouard Theis. Trocmé's daughter, Nelly Trocmé Hewett, wrote to me, "My father never had the opportunity to meet him,"[21] and André Chouraqui responded to my query in the following fashion: "I don't know if he knew André Trocmé personally. We never spoke about him."[22]

I have spent time ascertaining whom Camus knew on the plateau Vivarais-Lignon for the obvious reason that what Camus knew about what was going on there during his stay was in large measure predicated upon whom he knew in the area. Despite Lottman's claims, Camus was fully aware of the violent resistance activity in and around Le Chambon-sur-Lignon. Oscar Rosowsky, Jean Bouix, and Pierre Fayol all confirm this. Fayol and Camus were friends who, as Todd points out, even listened to the BBC together in Panelier.[23] In fact, despite the generally held view that Camus took no part in Resistance activity until after he left the plateau in late 1943, there are at least two reasons to believe that his Resistance work began somewhat earlier, while he lived in Panelier. The first is an August 31, 1944, letter to Francine in which he writes: "I joined the Resistance . . . I worked in the Haute-Loire region and then immediately after in Paris, with Pia, in the Combat sector." The second, as Gérard Bollon points out, is that his false papers, in the name of Albert Mathé, are dated May 20, 1943.[24]

19. Chouraqui, *L'Amour fort comme la mort*, 242.
20. Philip Hallie, "Camus's Hug," *The American Scholar* 64 (1995): 433.
21. Letter from Nelly Trocmé Hewett to author, August 12, 2001.
22. Letter from André Chouraqui to author, October 10, 1999.
23. Todd, *Albert Camus: une vie*, 320.
24. Ibid., 365. Bollon, *Les séjours d'Albert Camus*, 29.

Even Philip Hallie wonders about what Camus knew concerning the nonviolent resistance in the village.[25] Yet there were Jewish people staying everywhere on the plateau, even in Panelier, and Camus was in frequent contact with André Chouraqui, whose response to me makes it clear that Camus was as well informed about the nonviolent resistance (sheltering of potential victims of the Nazis) as he was about the violent resistance: "Albert Camus had always known about the resistance that Pastors Theis and Trocmé conducted in Le Chambon-sur-Lignon."[26]

Whatever Camus knew, whomever he knew on the plateau, he was alone, sick, and isolated from his wife, his friends, and the Algerian landscape he loved so well. His sense of exile and its ramifications surface everywhere; in his *Notebooks*, for example, he writes: "Four months of ascetic and solitary life. The will, the mind gain from it. But the heart?" (77) In this vein, it is significant that Camus would send out to be published a section of the major text he was working on. "Les Exilés dans la peste"[27] is a very close early draft of what would become the first chapter of part 2 of *The Plague*. This text, which begins, "In short, the time of the epidemic was above all a time of exile,"[28] defines the plague in terms of isolation. Here it is difficult not to see the sealing off of France from North Africa on November 11, 1942, which abruptly cut Camus off from his wife, family, and friends: "One of the most striking consequences of the closing of the gates was in fact the sudden separation that it imposed upon people who were not prepared for it. Mothers, children, spouses, lovers who a few days beforehand believed they were undertaking only a temporary separation."[29] One reads easily in the text Camus' personal feeling of exile in France as well as his sense

25. Hallie, "Camus's Hug," 434.

26. Letter from André Chouraqui to author, October 10, 1999.

27. "Les Exilés dans la peste," in *Théâtre, Récits, Nouvelles*, ed. Roger Quilliot (Paris: Gallimard, Bibliothèque de la Pléiade, 1962), 1951–59.

28. Ibid., 1951.

29. Ibid.

of cosmic exile: "Therefore everyone had to be content living from day to day, confronting the heavens alone."[30]

⌒

The Plague, a long prose narration Camus called a "chronicle" rather than a novel, literally tells the story of an outbreak of the disease in the 1940s in the city of Oran. His chronicle has physical, social, and metaphysical significance. The epigraph from Daniel Defoe immediately signals the allegorical nature of the text: "It is as reasonable to represent one kind of imprisonment by another, as it is to represent anything that really exists by that which [does not]."[31] The chronicle has a literal level, the fictional plague in Oran in 194–, which is an allegorical representation of the 1940–44 German occupation of France (often referred to by the French as "the brown plague"). Camus' story is also an allegorical portrayal of the human condition, stressed in a series of explicit statements carefully placed throughout the text ("Each of us has the plague." "What's natural is the microbe." "What does that mean—'plague'? Just life; no more than that." [1423, 1424, 1470; 229, 277]) and in the intense epic quality of the narrative, which refers repeatedly to some of the thirty-odd plagues throughout recorded history.

At each of these levels, Camus succeeds in depicting the themes of separation, exile, and isolation as central, just as the word "imprisonment" in the epigraph suggests. Repeatedly, during his stay in Panelier, he writes in his *Notebooks* that this is precisely what he intends to do: "Novel. Do not put 'The Plague' in the title. But something like 'The Prisoners.'" "Make the theme of separation the great theme of the novel" (41, 80). There are images of isolation on

30. Ibid., 1958.
31. Ibid., 1213. Albert Camus, *The Plague* (New York: Modern Library, 1948), ii. All references to *The Plague* are to this French edition: *La Peste*, in *Théâtre, Récits, Nouvelles*, 1211–1472. Translations are taken from the Modern Library edition and are amended when necessary; amended portions appear in brackets within the quotation in the text. Subsequent citations of the novel appear parenthetically in the text following the quotations; the page number of the French text precedes the page number of the English text.

every page of his narrative. One of the characters in the novel, Tarrou, sums up the fate of those who were totally unprepared for deprivation when he writes in his notebooks: "but worst of all is that they're forgotten and they know it" (1414; 217).

On the level of the German occupation of France, which is the level of interest in the present study, it is difficult not to personalize the text. Camus' *Notebooks* and many of the letters he wrote while on the plateau show how much of what he was experiencing has been transposed into the novel. Rieux's comment in the novel that the inhabitants "were wasting away emotionally as well as physically" (1363; 163), is close, even in image, to Camus' remark to Pierre and Marianne Fayol regarding the "slow crumbling away of the love of separated beings."[32] Even the abrupt November 11, 1942, closing of the door to Algeria that Camus indicates in his *Notebooks* with "like rats!" has its fictional counterpart as the last line of part 1 of the novel: "The telegram ran: *Proclaim a state of plague stop close the town*" (1267; 59). Part 2 then begins with a lightly edited version of "Les Exilés dans la peste," which Camus published while living on the plateau. Finally, Camus' post–November 11, 1942, journal entry—"An excessive use of Eurydice in the literature of the 1940s. It's because never before have so many lovers been separated" (56)—makes its way thematically into the mythological center of his tale of separation and exile when, as recorded in Tarrou's notebooks, the story of Orpheus and Eurydice is presented in Gluck's *Orpheus* at the Opéra Municipal and the actor playing Orpheus dies on the stage of the plague.

Nonetheless, Camus responded firmly to Roland Barthes, who claimed to find in *The Plague* "the politics of solitude": "Compared to *The Stranger*, *The Plague* marks, without any possible argument, the transition from an attitude of solitary revolt to the recognition of a community whose struggles we must share."[33] Camus' lungs were

32. Todd, *Albert Camus: une vie*, 321.
33. Camus, "Lettre à Roland Barthes," in *Théâtre, Récits, Nouvelles*, 1965–66.

certainly bothering him in France but he remarks in his *Notebooks* that his intention is to present a collective phenomenon: "I want to express by means of the plague the suffocation that we all suffered from and the threatening atmosphere and exile in which we lived" (72). Perhaps this very feeling of exile helped to establish a collective sense and to create his bridge to others, even if the French had the more enviable position of being exiled at home. In any event, working like Rieux, the physician in the text and its narrator, Camus used what he saw himself, the accounts of other eyewitnesses, and various documents to write and rewrite his chronicle of the plague years.

To Barthes's additional charge that "*The Plague* establishes an anti-historical morality," Camus responded that, while the novel can be read on several levels, one of those levels obviously portrays "the struggle of the European resistance against Nazism."[34] The text bears Camus out copiously. The novel, which he refers to in his *Notebooks* as "the phony plague" (69), is much more than this, but certainly it is not any less. There are constant references to the Occupation and to everyday life under Nazi rule. The date, "194 . . ." (1217; 3) and "this brutal [invasion of the disease]" (1271; 62) are accompanied by dozens of allusions to wartime conditions in France. In addition to the hoarding of foodstuffs, the requisitioning of schools, the reruns of old films, the black market, the rationing of gasoline, and the long lines in front of stores, there are "the establishment of a curfew hour" [1356; 155]), "controlling . . . the food supply" (1281; 72), "reductions . . . in the use of electricity" (1281; 72), and "a system of patrols" (1281; 103).

At the same time, there are numerous unmistakable references to the Holocaust in France. The most consistently sustained Holocaust image is that of "the isolation camps" (1412; 214), which are set up for those suspected of having the disease. These are clear-

34. Ibid., 1965.

ly references to the entirely French-run internment camps in the south of France where foreign Jews were held under horrific conditions. There can be no doubt that Camus knew not only about the existence of the camps but also about the legal and illegal activities to evacuate children from them. He knew about these activities because André Chouraqui's organization, OSE, was heavily involved in them and many of the children were sheltered in and around the area of Le Chambon-sur-Lignon. An entry about *The Plague* made in his *Notebooks* while he was living in Panelier makes this abundantly clear: "A chapter on the parents isolated *in the camps*" (69).

In the text when Tarrou describes in his notebooks the camp he visited, however, there is good reason to believe that he is referring to Paris, not to the south of France. No French person, especially a Parisian, could read about this "camp located in the municipal stadium . . . on the outskirts of town" with its "sentries" and its "[cement] walls" separating two worlds "as alien to each other as two different planets" (1412; 214–15) without thinking of the Vélodrome d'Hiver. After the infamous July 16–17, 1942, roundup, when thousands of French police arrested 13,152 Jews (12,884 of whom, including roughly 4,000 children, would ultimately be sent to Auschwitz), the victims, now that "the sports fields had been requisitioned" (1412; 215), were held in this indoor sporting arena located in the 15th arrondissement.

Finally, just as so many foreign Jews in France went from the internment camps in the southern part of the country to Drancy and then to the death camps in the East, so too the image of the camp in *The Plague* moves from the south, to Paris, and comes ultimately to represent the extermination camps outside France. The trains taking the victims out of the city, and the reign of bureaucracy— "the punctual thuds of rubber stamps marking the rhythm of lives and deaths" (1367; 167)—imply the route taken by the seventy-six thousand Jews living in France who were deported to the death camps. The death camps themselves are evoked throughout the novel by the narrator's references to "crematorium [ovens]" (1361, 1410; 161, 212), and the mass killing of Jews by "wild stories going round about the burials" (1357; 156), and by burial scenes such as the following: "men and women were flung into the death-pits indiscriminately [without any concern whatsoever for decency]" (1360; 159). Consistently throughout the novel, Camus insists on the solitude, isolation, and exile of the victims of the plague. Forty years before Primo Levi wrote the following sentence, Camus had it right: "We felt forgotten, like the condemned left to die in the medieval *oubliettes*."[35]

There are many traces of the plateau in the text. Although the general meaning of *The Plague* necessarily transcends any particulars regarding the plateau, it is important to recognize the marks of the area that Camus left in the text, either deliberately or unwittingly. Consider first the names of the characters. During the 1970s, Roger Darcissac (the director of the public school in Le Chambon-sur-Lignon during World War II) told Herbert Lottman that several names were of local origin: Paneloux comes from Panelier, Dr. Rieux from Dr. Paul Riou, and Grand was the name of a peasant friend of Camus who lived in Panelier.[36] Olivier Todd suggests that the name Rambert might have been derived from Montrambert (my Rambert?), a lower-class section of Saint-Etienne.[37]

Joseph Grand, like four other major characters (Rambert, Paneloux, Tarrou, and Rieux), is a man living alone, as Camus makes clear in an entry in his *Notebooks* written while he lived in Panelier: "In practice, there are only men who are alone in the novel" (80). Like Rieux and Rambert specifically, he is separated from the woman he loves. Furthermore, like all these characters, to one degree or

35. Primo Levi, *The Drowned and the Saved* (New York: Random House, 1988), 103.
36. Lottman, *Albert Camus: A Biography*, 274; 704.
37. Todd, *Albert Camus: une vie*, 321.

another, either ironically or profoundly, Grand shares traits with the author and, like them, also joins the "sanitary squads," voluntary teams of those willing, at the risk of their lives, to fight the plague. Something else that binds these men together despite their differences is the consistent downplaying of heroism throughout the narrative. Rambert remarks, "I don't believe in heroism" (1349, 149), and Rieux concurs: "Heroism and sanctity don't really appeal to me" (1425; 231). The narrator makes this a veritable leitmotif by insisting on the naturalness, logic, and ordinariness of fighting the plague. What is needed and sought are health, not salvation, men, not saints, and the practice of a simple, everyday morality. Those who attempt to transcend this level (Paneloux and Tarrou) die, while those who did not (Rambert, Grand, and Rieux) survive the plague.

This simple morality of ordinary people doing the right thing is illustrated by Joseph Grand from the first time he appears in the text. A clerk in the Municipal Office who speaks a very simple language but "seemed always to have trouble in finding his words" (1229; 17), Grand cuts down the would-be suicide Cottard and saves his life. When Rieux says they have to find someone to watch over Cottard for the night, Grand replies: "I can stay with him. I can't say I really know him, but [we have to help one another]" (1230; 19). In this novel where heroism resides in the secondary position "just after, never before, the noble claim of happiness" (1329; 126), it is precisely because of Grand's ordinariness—he had "all the attributes of insignificance" (1251; 41) and "had nothing of the hero about him" (1326; 122)—that Rieux, if compelled to choose the hero of the narrative, would choose Grand, "this insignificant and obscure hero" (1329; 126).

By his self-effacement, his ordinariness, and his kindness to strangers, Grand represents the rescuers of the plateau, the average people of the area who, like Grand, by their "small daily efforts" (1329; 127), very unself-consciously simply do what needs to be done. Grand prefigures the rescuers in Pierre Sauvage's brilliant documentary *Weapons of the Spirit* who cannot understand "all the fuss" and, like Georgette Barraud, repeatedly insist that what they did was natural and human, nothing more, nothing less: "Everything was just so natural that we don't understand why people would make such a fuss about it. It simply happened." The character's name, "Grand," is at once ironic because he, like the great majority of rescuers in the area, certainly comes from *"les petites gens"* ("ordinary people"), and fitting because he found the courage to practice the simple ethic of helping one's neighbor. Like the rescuers on the plateau, Grand "had the courage of [his] good feelings . . . [and with his natural good will] said yes without the slightest hesitation" (1252, 1326; 43, 123).

Todd's suggestion, in his biography of Camus, that the name "Rambert" might be derived from Montrambert is particularly fruitful, for "My Rambert" *("Mon Rambert")* links the character to the author and allows us to see just how closely Camus can be identified with this personage. Camus' position on the plateau resembles that of the journalist Rambert, who is trapped in Oran when the gates of the city are unexpectedly closed. Each is exiled, trapped away from home, far from the woman he loves, and each tries unsuccessfully to escape. Rambert claims that he has no connections with Oran—"[I'm a stranger in this city]" (1286; 77)—tries to escape on several occasions, and seems to want out at any cost; yet on the night before he is to make another attempt to escape, he decides to stay. When Rieux tells him that there is no shame in pursuing his happiness, Rambert responds that "it may be shameful to be happy by oneself. . . . I know that I belong here whether I want it or not. This business is everybody's business" (1387; 188). In addition to recalling Daniel Trocmé's words, written on September 11, 1942, to explain to his parents why he has chosen to go to Le Chambon ("I have chosen this adventure, not because it's an adventure, but so that I would not be ashamed of myself"), Rambert's

words echo those of Marguerite Roussel, a Catholic woman interviewed in *Weapons of the Spirit* who hid a Jewish family during the
war: "We all felt affected by what was going on . . . All of us were
threatened. So it was important to work together." It is not, then,
simply the feeling of exile that Rambert shares with his creator, but
far more importantly, deep ethical concerns born of a sudden or
growing awareness of human solidarity. In addition, Rambert is the
only character who, like Camus, survives the plague and goes back
apprehensively to the woman from whom he has been separated.
No wonder Camus told Roger Quilliot that Rambert was the character to whom he felt closest.[38]

When the Catholic priest, Father Paneloux, first appears in the
chronicle, Rieux asks him what he makes of this business about the
rats. "'Oh, I suppose it's an epidemic they've been having.' The Father's eyes were smiling behind his big round glasses" (1229; 16).
We soon find out that the "smiling eyes" suggest Paneloux's certitude that the plague demonstrates "the truth" of his religious beliefs. This need for proof and tendency to doubt follow Paneloux
from his first words in the novel to the last two words in the narrative that refer to him, describing him, ironically, as a "doubtful case"
(1408; 211). Camus had originally envisioned that Paneloux would
lose his faith during the plague: "A young priest loses his faith when
confronted with the black pus that flows from the wounds."[39]

In any event, Paneloux's first sermon is a rigorous, traditional,
and dogmatic explanation and justification of the plague: "Calam-
ity has come to you, my brethren," he says, "and, my brethren, you
deserved it" (1294; 86–87). Of divine origin and punitive character,
the plague has been sent to humble the proud and enlighten the
blind. Paneloux preaches penitence and acceptance of the plague as

38. Roger Quilliot, *The Sea and Prisons: A Commentary on the Life and Thought of
Albert Camus*, trans. Emmett Parker (University: University of Alabama Press, 1970),
143n.

39. Camus, *Carnets*, May 1935–February 1942, 230.

a justifiable form of punishment inflicted by God upon a sinful and culpable humanity. His sermon is reminiscent of those commonly delivered in France during the Occupation, sermons in which humility, culpability, and resignation to the "plague" were stressed. These conservative sermons fit perfectly with the politics of Vichy and inspired a spirit of resignation, even collaboration, rather than resistance to "the brown plague."

But, as Rieux points out when Paneloux joins the "sanitary squads": Paneloux is "better than his sermon" (1340; 138). While fighting the plague, he watches a child die. This "unbearable spectacle" (1395; 196) transforms his vision and lies at the heart of his second sermon, which is far more modest in tone and substance than the earlier one. Now the priest uses the first person "we" rather than the accusatory "you" of the first sermon. Paneloux had already told Rieux, just after the death of Judge Othon's child, that "perhaps we should love what we cannot understand" (1395; 196). Now he distinguishes between what is comprehensible and what is incomprehensible in respect to the Creator: "Thus we had apparently [necessary evil], and apparently [useless evil]; we had Don Juan cast into hell, and a child's death. For while it is right that a libertine should be struck down, we [do not understand the suffering of children]" (1400; 201). He pushes this idea still further: "My brothers, [the moment has come]. We must believe everything or deny everything. And who among you . . . would dare to deny everything" (1400; 202)? The traditional Christian who gave the first sermon has transformed himself into a Christian existentialist: for Paneloux, as for Kierkegaard, the act of faith is radically opposed to certitude; faith is indeed the crucifixion of reason. Paneloux follows his logic to his death: struck down by what probably is the plague, he dies without accepting medical help. The sickness was sent by God; it is therefore His will. A priest cannot consult a doctor because the doctor impedes the will of God by fighting against death. It was with good reason that Camus considered *The Plague* "the most anti-Christian of [his] books,"[40] for here he explicitly denounces Christianity, as he wrote earlier in his *Notebooks*, as "a doctrine of injustice" (112).

From the time he first arrived in Le Chambon-sur-Lignon on May 27, 1934, André Trocmé was known for his sermons. On that day, he presented his pacifist dogma: "No government can force us to kill; we have to find the means of resisting Nazism without killing people."[41] From that day forward, he was renowned for the originality, clarity, and precision of his thought and the power of his delivery. An active pacifist, he was at all times, before, during, and after World War II, a liberal antitotalitarian who promoted forgiveness, reconciliation, and peace. As Daniel Lys, pastor in Le Chambon-sur-Lignon from 1950 to 1962, writes: "Trocmé revived a pietistic parish with a transfusion of Social Christianity, with the emphasis clearly placed on pacifism."[42]

In his study of the sermons of the pastors on the plateau Vivarais-Lignon from 1940 to 1944, François Boulet finds a clear break between sermons up to July 1942 and those after that date. During the former period, according to Boulet, the sermons more or less conformed, if not to the dictates of the Vichy regime, at least to what the person of Marshal Pétain represented. They, therefore, contained the message of humility, humiliation, collective responsibility for the defeat of France, and the need for a moral and intellectual recovery. After the Vel d'Hiv roundup in July 1942, Boulet maintains, there is a radical rupture with Vichy and a reaffirmation of philo-Semitism in the sermons on the plateau. This break with Vichy becomes even more pronounced after the arrest of André Trocmé, Edouard Theis, and Roger Darcissac in February 1943. At this point, the summit of spiritual resistance on the plateau is reached.

40. Camus, *Théâtre, Récits, Nouvelles*, 1978.
41. Menut, "André Trocmé, un violent vaincu par Dieu," 390.
42. Ibid., 389.

Although Boulet seems to put Trocmé and Theis in a small group of those who were suspicious of Vichy and of conformism to its dictates from the very beginning, he maintains simultaneously that until the summer of 1942, that is, during all the time that anti-Jewish legislation was being promulgated and enacted by Vichy, there was, a few exceptions aside, a long silence on the plateau, a silence to which Boulet connects Trocmé when he cites him claiming on August 16, 1942, a month after Vel d'Hiv, "I could no longer remain silent."[43] This is wrong. Although the number of refugees in Le Chambon-sur-Lignon did increase greatly during the summer of 1942, Jews were already being hidden on the plateau years before that and Trocmé was in contact with groups working in the internment camps in the south of France, arranging such refuge in the area of Le Chambon-sur-Lignon more than a year and a half before the Vel d'Hiv roundup.

Although we have only one of Trocmé's wartime sermons from this period before summer 1942 and none of the notes he preached from, Le Chambon-sur-Lignon researcher Annik Flaud remarks that "preaching for the welcoming [of foreigners on the plateau] did not necessarily have to be done from the pulpit. There were neighborhood meetings, scouts [who often served as guides to the refugees who had to hide out], Bible study meetings, catechesis and presbytery councils."[44] Furthermore, Georges Menut maintains that Trocmé's sermons "became more important during the war. . . . without knowing who took notes and passed them on, we do know that quotations from his sermons made their way into the internment camps in the south of France and raised morale there."[45] It seems unlikely that this would have been the case had Trocmé been silent regarding the treatment of Jews by the Nazis and the Vichy government.

43. François Boulet, "Les prédications des pasteurs," in Bolle et al., *Le Plateau Vivarais-Lignon,* 369.
44. Annik Flaud, letter to author, May 6, 2002.
45. Menut, "André Trocmé, un violent vaincu par Dieu," 389.

The one sermon we do have from that period, Trocmé and Theis's June 23, 1940, sermon, delivered one day after the armistice was signed with the Germans, not only before the deportation of any Jews but three months before the beginning of the anti-Jewish legislation promulgated by Vichy, contains words of resistance against any practices by the government that violate the Gospels. This sermon contains elements of both sermons given by Paneloux in *The Plague*. Although written in a much less harsh and unyielding tone than Paneloux's first sermon, it too refers to the people of Israel and contains the same message of culpability, humility, penitence, and, in its own way, hope and comfort. At the same time, however, Trocmé and Theis advocate resistance, as does Paneloux in his second sermon when he notes that "[we must not] listen to certain moralists who told us [that we have to get] on our knees and give up the struggle" (1403; 205).

Trocmé and Theis's sermon is, in fact, far more detailed regarding resistance against the Nazis than is Paneloux's second sermon which, even if it touches on resistance, is concerned more with understanding the plague in the context of the Christian God than in fighting it. We should not forget, however, that Paneloux has been working for the "sanitary squads" ever since he delivered his first sermon. In their June 23, 1940, sermon, Trocmé and Theis are intent on telling parishioners what has not been lost, "Gospel truths," "the Word of God," "faith," and what they need to do in the wake of the German takeover: avoid confusing humiliation with discouragement; avoid the temptation to scapegoat and to blame "one's fellow citizens or foreign people"; avoid yielding to anything "contrary to the commands of the Gospel." In short, they urge their parishioners to recognize that Nazism is an extreme form of anti-Christianity and that one must never actively collaborate with it or even be somehow coerced into "a passive submission to totalitarian ideology." Trocmé and Theis define their spiritual resistance toward the end of the sermon in quasi-aphoristic terms: "The duty of

Christians is to use the weapons of the Spirit to resist the violence brought to bear on their consciences . . . We will resist whenever our adversaries try to force us to act against the commands of the Gospel. We will do so without fear, but also without pride and without hatred."[46] This powerful and unequivocal message of resistance may have been the first public declaration of resistance to the Nazis in France. It also coheres well with Trocmé's notion of nonviolent resistance as he defines it in his "Mémoires": "Nonviolence is not a theory superimposed on reality; it's an itinerary that one explores day after day in common prayer and obedience to the directives of the Holy Spirit."[47]

There is an additional link between Paneloux and Trocmé, one obvious to anyone who either knew Trocmé personally or has read his unpublished memoirs. Just as in *The Plague*, where, toward the end of the epidemic, there are several unexpected and absurd deaths, so too on the plateau toward the end of "the brown plague," there were at least two totally absurd, unexpected, and completely preventable deaths, one of which was that of Pastor Trocmé's fourteen-year-old son, Jean-Pierre, who accidentally killed himself in August 1944.[48]

In his memoirs, more than twenty years after this tragic accident, Trocmé explains how this death of a child, as in the case of Paneloux, completely transformed his faith. Like Paneloux, he does not lose his faith in God but his transformation is far more extreme. Gone, for example, is the old faith in security and Providence ("The Eternal was the one who looked after me . . . The Heavens were benevolent"): "I lost the faith, at least the confidence in a God who accompanies me and protects me from all evil." Like Paneloux, he

46. André Trocmé and Edouard Theis, "Message des deux pasteurs du Chambon à leur paroisse (Dimanche 23 juin 1940)," in Bolle et al., *Le Plateau Vivarais-Lignon*, 597–99.
47. André Trocmé, "Mémoires," 357.
48. The other was that of Madeleine "Manou" Barraud, who was accidentally shot to death by a friend in July 1944.

went right back into the pulpit to preach "a Gospel of wager": "I was in the pulpit. . . . I preached the Gospel, not the Gospel of childish confidence, but a more severe Gospel, more pared down, a Gospel of wager, a Gospel turned toward the future." Unable to pray for a very long time ("incapable . . . of having a dialogue with a God who remains silent"), Trocmé explains that he has never gotten over this tragedy and continues to live with "an incurable wound," "an insurmountable obstacle," "unthinkable memories, horrors that one cannot evoke without the fear of losing one's mind." His "new" God suffers along with humanity ("a God totally immersed in the sufferings of the creation") but cannot protect him. Trocmé claims to have come to see the human condition in ways similar to those of Sartre and Camus: "Insignificant Playthings, that's what we were. . . . We are cast into the world subjected to absurd, chaotic circumstances, that's what life is. . . . Without knowing it, I had joined Sartre and Camus, both of whom were still unknown at the time."[49]

As a Protestant pastor, Trocmé is thus comparable with the chronicle's ecclesiastic, Paneloux. As a pacifist, he is tied to Tarrou. The first time Tarrou appears, he is watching "the [final] convulsions of a rat dying on the step [at his feet]" (1225; 12) and, until his own death at the end of the novel, Tarrou dedicates himself to alleviating suffering and to the nearly impossible task of not spreading the plague. Camus also gave lots of thought to nonviolence. He joined the Resistance because he discovered that he hated violence less than the institutions of violence. In a March 1952 letter to Etienne Benoit, he writes: "I studied . . . the theory of nonviolence and I'm not far from concluding that it represents a truth worthy of being taught by example. But, to do so, one would need a greatness that I don't have."[50] Tarrou has that "greatness" and it links him to Trocmé, who believes that one must resist violence but only with "the weapons of the spirit." Here is one of Tarrou's formulations of

49. André Trocmé, "Mémoires," 439–40; 538; 8.
50. Todd, *Albert Camus: une vie*, 456.

his pacifism: "I [decided to reject everything] which, directly or indirectly, for good reasons or for bad, [kills or justifies that one can kill]. . . . I definitely refused to kill" (1423–24; 228–29).

So, like Trocmé who, with others, arranged for refuge in his parish, Tarrou creates and organizes the "sanitary squads." What he tells Cottard is similar to Trocmé's admonition to his parishioners: "do try at least not to propagate the microbe deliberately" (1347; 146). Tarrou also expresses the same confidence in human beings to do good that emanated from Trocmé's pulpit. When Rieux, upon learning that Paneloux had joined the "sanitary squads," tells Tarrou that he is glad to know that Paneloux is "better than his sermon," Tarrou replies: "[Everyone is] like that . . . It's only a matter of giving them the chance. . . . That's my job in life—giving people chances" (1340; 138).

More striking still is Tarrou and Trocmé's total commitment always to side with the victims. Tarrou remarks to Rieux: "I decided to take, in every predicament, the victims' side, so as to reduce the damage done" (1424–25; 230). This was obviously the case of Trocmé and Theis, who risked their lives, were arrested, and finally were forced to go into hiding, all to protect individuals from the Nazis. Tarrou wonders if he might become "a saint without God" (1425; 230) and spends his life "[seeking peace in the service of others]" (1457; 263). In many ways, including this anguished quest for peace in the service of others, Tarrou is a secular version of Trocmé who, during the last weeks of the war, when Frenchmen were finally getting revenge and Germans were being assassinated everywhere, still taught the absolute uselessness of all hatred and the need for forgiveness. Accompanied by August Bohny and, as of Easter 1946, Howard Schomer, Trocmé now preached on Sundays in the nearby German prisoner of war camp, where he offered the opportunity to repent in hope of ending all cycles of vengeance.

Whereas Tarrou wondered if he might become a saint without God, Rieux aspires only to be a man: "Heroism and sanctity don't really appeal to me, I imagine. What interests me is being a man" (1425; 231). Unlike Paneloux, for whom the plague, at least initially, means the absolute confirmation of his theological views, Rieux, whose vision is solely terrestrial, can find certitude only in doing his job: "There lay certitude; there, in the daily round" (1248; 38). The name "Rieux" came from the name of Dr. Paul Riou of Le Chambon-sur-Lignon. But the character himself, if based on a doctor in Le Chambon-sur-Lignon, was more than likely based on Dr. Roger Le Forestier. Whether Camus knew Le Forestier personally has not been established, but given Le Forestier's popularity in the village and the fact that he practiced the same pneumothorax therapy that Camus received in Saint-Etienne, it is highly unlikely that Camus did not know of him.[51] Both Roger Le Forestier and his fictional counterpart Bernard Rieux are doctors committed to fighting "the plague" and to waging war on human suffering. But there are very obvious differences between them. Rieux is a nonbeliever who survives the plague, whereas Le Forestier was a fervent Christian who had worked in Africa with Albert Schweitzer before coming to Le Chambon-sur-Lignon. Unfortunately, he was arrested in Le Puy and murdered in Saint Genis-Laval. At all times throughout "the plague," like André Trocmé, Rieux was there "[to] bear witness in favor of those plague-stricken people" (1471; 278). Each would have told the other what Rieux told Paneloux: "We're working side by side for something that unites us—beyond blasphemy and prayers. And it's the only thing that matters" (1395; 197).

During the time Camus spent on the plateau Vivarais-Lignon, he worked on *The Plague*. He was familiar with the Resistance in the Lyon area through Pascal Pia and René Leynaud and in the area of Le Chambon-sur-Lignon through Pierre Fayol. At the same time, as André Chouraqui confirms, Camus knew about the rescue work of

51. Annik Flaud, fax to author, September 3, 1999; Todd, *Albert Camus: une vie*, 795 n. 15.

André Trocmé, Edouard Theis, and others on the plateau. He was also acquainted with other individuals in the area, such as Jean Bouix, who were involved in clandestine rescue work. In addition, there are many clear allusions to World War II, the German occupation of France, and the Holocaust in *The Plague,* which ostensibly treats a disease-stricken city. It is abundantly clear, as Camus himself states against certain critics of this work, that among other things, *The Plague* portrays allegorically the European struggle against Nazism.

From the time of the book's publication, its author has been consistently criticized by such people as Simone de Beauvoir, Jean-Paul Sartre, Francis Jeanson, and Roland Barthes precisely for using the plague to allegorize the German occupation of France. This is a serious criticism even if it has been advanced primarily by people intent on denigrating Camus' book. A plague is essentially a nonhuman phenomenon; wars are willfully man-made. Even when we speak of war as a disease, we recognize that it is caused by humans. The French were not fighting a nonhuman epidemic between the years 1940 and 1944. They were fighting other men. When this fact is blurred, good and evil become easily definable, characters can be taken out of their specific historical situation, and the question of violence is avoided, thereby enabling the characters to keep their hands clean. Even a very sympathetic critic, such as John Weightman, sees this contradiction and criticizes Camus for claiming in interviews that "the plague also symbolizes war." Weightman maintains, against the author of the text himself, that "*La Peste* contains no internal reference to war." Most recently, Tony Judt has come to Camus' defense, justifying reading his chronicle as "an allegory of the occupation years."[52]

On the plateau Vivarais-Lignon, there were active nonviolent and

52. John Weightman, "The Outsider," *The New York Review of Books,* January 15, 1998, 29. Tony Judt, "On *The Plague*," *The New York Review of Books,* November 29, 2001, 8.

violent factions resisting both Nazism, "the brown plague," and Vichy, "the grey plague." Because of the emphasis in Philip Hallie's *Lest Innocent Blood Be Shed* and Pierre Sauvage's *Weapons of the Spirit,* the area is primarily known for its nonviolent resistance. This is perhaps as it should be. There was no other nonviolent communal effort on this scale for this length of time anywhere else in Occupied Europe during the Holocaust. But the village's postwar reputation for nonviolence has eclipsed the violent activities that went on there during the Occupation. This is a highly unusual situation because, throughout France, just the opposite has been true: massive recognition for the Resistance, little, if any, recognition of rescue. In this regard, Marianne Fayol remarks that her husband, Pierre Fayol, decided to write *Le Chambon-sur-Lignon sous L'Occupation (1940–1944). Les résistances locales, l'aide interalliée, l'action de Virgina Hall (O.S.S.)* to point out what everyone had forgotten: "Listen, the book about Le Chambon-sur-Lignon was written because everyone knew about Le Chambon-sur-Lignon, the village that saved 5,000 Jews, and everyone had forgotten Le Chambon-sur-Lignon, the village that was part of the Resistance."[53] The *maquis* worked in the area with Fayol as one of its leaders, and there were Jewish freedom fighters in the surrounding forests. While Trocmé was absent from Le Chambon-sur-Lignon toward the end of the war, armed resistance in the area increased (as it did elsewhere in France at the same time) and some of the students from the Ecole Nouvelle Cévenole joined the underground and took part in sabotage activities.

Atypically, the nonviolent resisters and the violent Resistance were sometimes in contact with one another in the area of Le Chambon-sur-Lignon. I am not thinking particularly here of André Trocmé and Edouard Theis, even though Trocmé and Fayol had an obvious respect for one another. In his "Mémoires," Trocmé remarks that Fayol, who was "his friend," had "a great nobility of character." "He came to see me often," continues Trocmé, "and why not?

53. Unpublished interview with Barbara Barnett (July 1994).

We both had moderate views. I believed it was insane to attack German detachments in the area. Doing so would only incite reprisals. He agreed."[54] The case of the Eyraud family, however, shows how these two groups were often intertwined and to some degree how they worked together. Madame Eyraud ran a *pension* in which many children and young adults were hidden during the Occupation. At the same time, her husband, Léon "Père Noël" Eyraud, was a leader in the *maquis*. Their daughter writes that "the house became the rallying place for the young members of the *maquis*." She also explains how her father took forceful steps to prevent the useless killing of Germans in the area: "I remember the day when he learned about the plan of some young members of the *maquis* to come and machine-gun convalescing German soldiers who would go swimming at the beach . . . his goal was not only to protect the village but defenseless men as well."[55]

There can be no doubt that *maquis* leaders like Pierre Fayol and Léon Eyraud realized that the fate of the village and of the nonviolent rescue going on there was to a large extent dependent upon how they conducted business. Had they killed Germans indiscriminately, there would certainly have been massive retaliations on both the violent and nonviolent contingents in the area. As if to prove Fayol, Trocmé, and Eyraud right, Robert Gildea gives an example of recklessness by the Resistance that resulted in a massacre in Touraine in 1944, and Adam Nossiter relates the story of the horrific reprisal by the Nazis in Tulle for an attack by the Resistance on a nearby German garrison. Both of these tragedies serve as the grimmest of reminders of what might have happened on the plateau Vivarais-Lignon or anywhere else in Occupied France in retaliation for the murder of German soldiers.[56] Thus, on the plateau, violent and nonviolent groups

54. André Trocmé, "Mémoires," 417.

55. Aline Caritey, "Un chef local: Léon Eyraud," in Bolle et al., *Le Plateau Vivarais-Lignon*, 494; 495.

56. Robert Gildea, *Marianne in Chains*, 12; Adam Nossiter, *The Algeria Hotel:*

actually worked to insure the safety of the village and of all the active resistance groups, violent and nonviolent, that operated there. Even when they operated separately, military and spiritual resisters, with believers and nonbelievers in each group, worked for something that united them beyond their differences.

How, then, can fighting disease function allegorically or metaphorically to represent the struggle against Nazism? *The Plague* reproduces the dominant form of resistance, rescue, which was taking place in the area where Camus was composing his narration. As on the plateau, in *The Plague* believers and nonbelievers work together toward that goal. Whether one was fighting a disease or rescuing Jews and others from the Nazis, the aim was the same: "The essential thing was to save the greatest possible number of persons from dying" (1325; 122). On the plateau, as well as in the text, this goal was mainly achieved nonviolently. People risked their lives on the plateau to save potential victims without killing the perpetrators of this violence, and their subdued heroism shines forth in the book's characters.

But *The Plague* does more than simply mirror the nonviolent resistance on the plateau. In a text ostensibly depicting the struggle against a disease, Camus represents allegorically the violent struggle against the Nazis also taking place on the plateau, thereby justifying, at a second level, his claim that the narrative portrays "the struggle of the European resistance against Nazism." Disease was certainly on Camus' mind as he wrote his chronicle in Panelier: he had come there in the hope of defeating his own tuberculosis; he was writing a work of fiction about a plague in Oran; when he moved to Paris in late 1943 and sent a Jewish woman to be hidden in the village, in his coded language to Pierre Fayol, he wrote that she suffered from "an hereditary infection."[57] Nazism was like

France, Memory and the Second World War (New York: Houghton Mifflin Company, 2001), 217–72.

57. Todd, *Albert Camus: une vie*, 335.

the plague that had to be defeated and all the main characters of the book, except Cottard, ultimately join the fight against it. Camus wrote in his *Notebooks:* "Plague. Everyone struggles against it—each in his own way. The only form of cowardice is to get down on one's knees before it" (107).

Dozens of allusions keep the reader aware of the fact that the text is allegorically about the 1940–44 German occupation of France, an occupation that also met with violent resistance, even if only by a very small fraction of French people. Camus represents this violent resistance with allusions to the Occupation and by reiterating that those who joined the "sanitary squads" "were risking their lives" (1325; 121): "[This work could be fatal]" (1319; 115), Rieux cautions, and Rambert tells Rieux: "[I would be able to risk my life again]; I took part in the Spanish Civil War" (1349; 149). Ramifications of fighting disease are like ramifications of resisting the Nazis, and death was a real possibility for those who resisted the plague both violently and nonviolently on the plateau Vivarais-Lignon.

The discussions between Tarrou and Rieux show two ways of being that reflect two different ways of fighting the plague. Tarrou is an absolutely nonviolent pacifist whose central quest is to "acquire peace of mind" (1236; 261) by becoming "a saint without God" (1425; 230). He is completely obsessed by all forms of the death penalty and he "denied [human beings] the right to condemn anyone whomsoever" (1457; 263). As Camus wrote of him in his *Notebooks* while on the plateau: "Tarrou is the man who can understand everything—and who suffers because of it. He can't judge anything" (70). As a result, he feels totally exiled: "once I'd definitively refused to kill, I doomed myself to an exile that can never end. I leave it to others to make history" (1424; 229). This painful expression of Tarrou's isolation once he became completely dedicated to nonviolence is mirrored in the memoirs and correspondence of André Trocmé who, with a handful of other nonviolent ministers, was exiled in his own country and within his own Church as a result of his total commitment to pacifism. From at least 1930 onward, because of his pacifism, his belief in conscientious objection, and his work with the European Fellowship of Reconciliation (Mouvement de la Réconciliation), Trocmé was labeled "a troublemaker" and "an anarchistic and difficult undesirable." His pastoral career was seriously compromised. At that time, one could not become a pastor in the Reformed Church of France without signing an agreement "not to campaign in favor of conscientious objection." One could be a conscientious objector but one could not communicate one's pacifist convictions to anyone, especially to the young. "No French parish of any importance," writes Trocmé, "would have dared to take responsibility for such a 'dangerous' pastor."[58] There was a serious effort to isolate and silence these conscientious objectors to keep their ideology from spreading. This explains how Trocmé was finally appointed, temporarily, to his isolated mountain village. But, with Theis and others, from 1940 to 1944, Trocmé did, in fact, "make history."

Rieux, on the other hand, is equally committed to the cause of justice and the struggle against human suffering but wants only to be a man and seems fully at home in his job. Is he the one who can judge? His "limited" aspirations and solely human perspective might suggest the broadening of options, the impossibility of sanctity, the dirtying of hands, and the necessity of violence in fighting "the plague." In this regard, Camus "quotes" Rieux toward the end of 1943 in his *Notebooks:* "Rieux: 'Every community in conflict needs men who kill and men who heal. I have chosen to heal'" (107). It is significant that Rieux became more nuanced in his creator's mind, for he never makes this simple dichotomy in the novel, thereby blurring an absolute distinction between violence and healing. From this perspective, Tarrou certainly resembles Trocmé in his embodiment of nonviolent rescue, whereas Rieux might possibly incarnate Fayol and the violent resistance.

58. André Trocmé, "Mémoires," 289; 303; 325–26.

With the heavy emphasis on rescue accompanied by suggestions of violent resistance, Camus faithfully represents the plateau and its diverse forms of resistance to the disease of Nazism. *The Plague* does not pose all the ethical problems and burdens of choice that the Occupation did, but it raises many of them and suggests others within its limited fictional framework. It is absurd to maintain that the novel projects "an attitude of nonintervention" and that "the notion of risk does not exist in *The Plague*."[59]

At the end of the narrative, Rieux claims that what we learn in a time of pestilence is that "there are more things to admire in men than to despise" (1471; 278). Most people who lived in Occupied Europe during the Nazi plague probably would not agree, but most of them did not spend fourteen or fifteen months of that time, as Camus did, in Panelier, on the plateau Vivarais-Lignon.

59. Gaëtan Picon, "Notes on *The Plague*," in *Camus, A Collection of Critical Essays*, ed. Germaine Brée (Englewood Cliffs, N.J.: Prentice-Hall, 1962), 150.

5 ⌣⌐

The Rescuers of Jews

The rescuers are hard to find in the great explosion of literature on the Holocaust. Those who concealed Jewish children and protected Jewish adults from the Nazis have themselves been hidden in the accounts of this horrific European genocide. For one thing, many rescuers died in the years immediately following the end of World War II, and others, like many of the Jews they rescued, simply wanted to forget the past and get on with their lives. Also, the great majority of rescuers did not come forth looking for recognition. Almost all accounts, in all countries, show that most rescuers do not think they did anything remarkable. Most rescuers believe that they simply did what any normal person would have done. With good reason, rescuers in countries where anti-Semitism was particularly virulent feared repercussions if it were to become known that they had hidden Jews during the war. Secrecy had become a way of life, a way of staying alive during the Holocaust for the rescuers and the rescued alike. Eva Fogelman found that "many rescuers retained the habit of secrecy even after secrecy was no longer necessary"[1] and many did so because they did not want their extended families to know to what extent they had endangered the

1. Eva Fogelman, *Conscience and Courage,* 73–74.

lives of their immediate families in an attempt to save the lives of strangers. In the late 1970s, however, when neo-Nazi groups asserted that "the Holocaust was a Zionist hoax," large numbers of rescuers, compelled by a moral responsibility to speak the truth of their past, came forward along with scores of survivors to refute this outrageous revisionism.[2]

It is not, however, just the attitude of the rescuers that explains their relative absence in the literature of the Holocaust. The point of view of others also accounted for little light being shed on rescuer activities, particularly in the first decades after the war. In France, as Julian Jackson points out, to cite a particular national example that persists to some degree even into our current century, "the wider public still resists the view that the Occupation might after all have contained heroes." Given the fact that the Occupation was such a national catastrophe, it is "more comforting to believe that all were guilty than that the honour of the nation was saved by a tiny minority."[3] More generally, many of the victims fear that studying the rescuers would detract from the horror of the Holocaust. Martin Gilbert remarks that, during the first few decades after the war, "understandably, Jewish writers wanted to tell the story of the suffering, the destruction, and the murder of loved ones, as well as of Jewish resistance and revolt."[4] Nechama Tec, one of the groundbreaking researchers on the rescuers, does not find "the prolonged silence" regarding the rescuers surprising: "It is only natural and expected that those who studied these tragic events focused first on the typical experience rather than the rare exception."[5] Both

2. Ibid., 302.

3. Julian Jackson, *France: The Dark Years*, 16, 631. See also Paul Thibaud: "La Culpabilité française," *Esprit* 168 (1991); "La République et ses héros: Le Gaullisme pendant et après la guerre," *Esprit* 198 (1994): 64–83; "Un temps de mémoire," *Le Débat* 96 (1996): 166–83.

4. Martin Gilbert, *The Righteous: The Unsung Heroes of the Holocaust* (New York: Henry Holt & Company, 2003), xvii.

5. Nechama Tec, *When Light Pierced the Darkness: Christian Rescue of Jews in Nazi-Occupied Poland* (New York: Oxford University Press, 1986), 5.

Martin Gilbert and Eva Fogelman met resistance when they began their research on the rescuers. "Enough is being written on Christian help to rescue Jews," replied one Polish-born Jew to Gilbert. "I feel that the focus is shifting away from the crimes."[6] This attitude was not unusual. Many survivors held it because they had received no help and remained bitter that so few non-Jews came to their defense. While explaining that "not all Holocaust survivors were so supportive of my work," Fogelman remarks: "Since so few non-Jews had helped them, many survivors doubted the rescuers' altruistic motivations. Many worried that by highlighting the courageous acts of a relative handful of individuals, I would obscure the essential fact that six million Jews were murdered."[7]

It is easy to understand such attitudes and fears, particularly during the first decades after World War II. How could one possibly contest them? Yet when, almost fifty years after the liberation of the camps, *Schindler's List,* to choose but one example, is reviled for having "distorted the meaning and lesson of the Holocaust by focusing on a Christian rescuer,"[8] it is time to ask why it is considered a distortion to present historically valid accounts from the period of the genocide and to analyze relationships therein other than the dominant perpetrator-victim dyad. To make a film about the exception—rescue—is not to negate the slaughter of the Jews by the Nazis, any more than a film about the French Resistance should be viewed as an effort to negate the more dominant role of French collaboration during the Occupation. If the survivor-child relationship is a legitimate field of analysis, as Art Spiegelman's graphic novel *Maus,* its most brilliant and terrifying exemplification, demonstrates, why is the survivor-rescuer dyad still so suspect? Every film about rescue, by its very nature, insists on the horrific fate that

6. Gilbert, *The Righteous,* xviii.
7. Fogelman, *Conscience and Courage,* xvii.
8. Peter Novick, *The Holocaust in American Life* (New York: Houghton Mifflin Co., 1999), 180. This is not Novick's view. He is citing others. See p. 325, n. 39.

potentially awaited all Jews in Occupied Europe. Furthermore, it is misleading to claim that to study the rescuers is an attempt to hide from the horror of the Holocaust. To argue that writing about rescue "colours the disaster with a rosy tinge and helps us to manage the unimaginable without having to look at its naked and ugly face" is particularly false and distasteful when we consider, for example, Daniel Trocmé's death in the gas chamber at Maidanek and the months that Madeleine Dreyfus, lice-infested and starving, spent in Bergen-Belsen.[9]

There is, finally, the claim that to write about the rescuers is to try to find some good in the heart of evil. But there is no evil in the act of saying "No" to the genocide of the Jews. Cynthia Ozick notes, with her characteristic lucidity and succinct prose, "The Holocaust happened *to* its victims. It did not happen *in* them. The victims were not the participants . . . they were separated from its meaning. They had clean hands. The perpetrators *are* the Holocaust; the victims stand apart."[10] Similarly, the rescuers had clean hands. They stood beside the Jews outside the Holocaust. They were not part of the proceedings. Ozick also singles out the rescuers in Le Chambon-sur-Lignon ("a whole village that would not implicate itself in evil") to insist that there "goodness separated itself from desecration." To study the rescuers, then, to use Ozick's term, is not to go looking for "spots of goodness on the rump of evil."

The Shoah refers to the annihilation of six million Jewish people. There is certainly no redeeming or positive message and no reassuring lesson to be extracted from that slaughter. As Cynthia Ozick has noted: "'Never Again' is not the message we get from the Holocaust. The message we get is that the Holocaust will replicate

---

9. The quotation is from Lawrence Langer, *Admitting the Holocaust* (New York: Oxford University Press, 1995), 3. When writing about Yad Vashem, it is cited with approbation by Tim Cole, *Selling the Holocaust: From Auschwitz to Schindler* (New York: Routledge, 2000), 172.

10. Cynthia Ozick, "Roundtable Discussion," in *Writing and the Holocaust,* ed. Berel Lang (New York: Holmes & Meier, 1988), 284.

itself. Once the restraints are down, the next time becomes easier; the next time will have a precedent and a model."[11] It will be the matter of this chapter, however, to ascertain whether something positive can be learned from those who not only refused to be part of this genocide but who risked their lives trying to save its potential victims. To be faithful to the Jewish proverb "In remembrance resides the secret of redemption," we must be certain to remember the rescuers. The verb "remember" has its surgical sense of putting things back together again and the acts of solidarity performed by the rescuers were part of the picture. These lights that shone only here and there in the overall darkness enable us to see and to find our way out of the labyrinth of blind hatred within which they were performed. In the war against the Jews, the rescuers represent the *Lamed Vav*, the thirty-six unknown Just Persons whose task is to do good for their fellow human beings and who, the Talmud says, are required for the survival of the world.

Israeli Prime Minister David Ben-Gurion proposed the establishment of Yad Vashem to reward the righteous and by an act of the Israeli parliament, the Knesset, this was accomplished on May 18, 1953. Situated in Jerusalem, Yad Vashem ("monument and name"), the Holocaust Martyrs' and Heroes' Remembrance Authority, is the official Israeli national institution for commemoration of the Holocaust. It is dedicated to research and education and houses in its archives approximately "fifty million pages of documents and testimonies in a variety of languages, over 100,000 photographs, and more than 600 documentary and feature films." Its adjoining library contains more than eighty thousand titles.[12]

By law, one of the functions of Yad Vashem is to perpetuate the memory of the righteous by, for example, granting them honorary

11. Ibid., 281.
12. Mooli Brog, "Yad Vashem," in *The Holocaust Encyclopedia*, ed. Walter Laqueur (New Haven, Conn.: Yale University Press, 2001), 697. I have drawn freely from Brog's entry, which covers pages 697–701.

Israeli citizenship. In 1962, the Avenue of the Righteous Among the Nations was dedicated and, since 1963, a commission has awarded the distinction of *Hasidei Umot Ha-olam* (literally "Righteous Ones Among the Nations of the World," but often reduced to "Righteous Among the Nations" or "Righteous Gentiles") to all non-Jews who, going beyond giving ordinary help, risked their lives to save Jewish people during the Shoah without receiving any reward for having done so.[13] It is virtually impossible to become a "Righteous Gentile" without being nominated by the specific individual or individuals one rescued.

How many people did in fact risk their lives to save Jews during the Shoah? The only certain answers are "far too few" and "only the tiniest fraction." Estimates vary. Some say only 0.01 percent, others 0.25 percent. Generally speaking, the highest estimate is 0.50 percent, which would mean that 99.5 percent of non-Jews did nothing at all to help Jews during the Holocaust. Harold Schulweis notes that "Holocaust scholars now estimate that there were between fifty thousand and five hundred thousand Christian rescuers."[14] Since the higher figure is ten times the lower one, these figures mean little other than, in either case, the figure is regrettably low, especially if, as Eva Fogelman says, there were "700 million people in Nazi-occupied territories."[15] In his epilogue to Wladyslaw Szpilman's *The Pianist,* a memoir of the Jewish composer's survival in Warsaw during the Holocaust, which was made into an award-winning film in 2003 by Roman Polanski, Wolf Biermann claims that "some three to four hundred thousand Poles risked their lives to save Jews." He points out that in 1999 when he wrote his epilogue, almost one-

13. On these points, see Nechama Tec, "Righteous Among the Nations," in *The Holocaust Encyclopedia,* 569–74.

14. Harold M. Schulweis, *For Those Who Can't Believe: Overcoming the Obstacles to Faith* (New York: Harper Collins Publishers, 1994), 152.

15. Fogelman, *Conscience and Courage,* xvi. Berel Lang estimates that figure at three hundred million. Lang, "Uncovering Certain Mischievous Questions about the Holocaust," 10.

third of the Righteous Gentiles were Polish, despite the fact that, "if you hid a Jew in France, the penalty was prison or a concentration camp, in Germany it cost you your life—but in Poland it cost the lives of your entire family."[16] The 21,758 "Righteous Among the Nations" designated by Yad Vashem as of January 1, 2007, do not begin to approximate either the total number of rescued Jews or the total number of "Righteous Gentiles," but rather simply reflect the material on rescue operations made available to Yad Vashem.

For a long time, rescuers were largely ignored in Israel. Malka Drucker reports that the rescuers living in Israel, nearly all Polish, many in poverty, were denied full government benefits and pensions because they were not Jewish. In 1985, however, the Israeli television show *Kolbotek* (the Israeli equivalent of *60 Minutes*) highlighted "the plight of rescuers in Israel, and after forty years the government corrected the injustice."[17] A special stipend was given to rescuers and a support group was eventually created for them by a Jewish woman living in Israel who had been rescued in Poland.[18] In January 1987, in a most unprecedented action, the Israeli parliament invited the rescuers living in Israel to attend a regular session of the Knesset and stood in unison in their honor.[19]

Around the same time, in 1986, a California rabbi, Harold Schulweis, established the Jewish Foundation for the Righteous (JFR) "to create a vehicle to provide financial and medical support to those aged and needy non-Jews who risked their lives to save Jews during the Holocaust and to develop educational programs centering on the Holocaust and the altruism and moral courage of the Chris-

16. Wolf Biermann, "Epilogue," in *The Pianist*, by Wladyslaw Szpilman (New York: Picador, 1999), 212. Today, in 2007, it's closer to a quarter than a third (6,004 Polish rescuers; 21,758 total Righteous Gentiles).

17. Gay Block and Malka Drucker, *Rescuers: Portraits of Moral Courage in the Holocaust* (New York: Holmes & Meier Publishers, 1992), 16.

18. Nechama Tec mentions that "the 'Righteous Among Nations' Awards are often accompanied by financial aid." In poor countries, like Poland, "practically all 'Righteous Christians' receive a modest pension." *When Light Pierced the Darkness*, 4.

19. Fogelman, *Conscience and Courage*, 304.

tian rescuer."[20] In addition to its educational programs and speakers bureau, "in 2004 the JFR provided monthly financial assistance to 1,600 aged and needy Righteous in 28 countries and made special grants to rescuers in Eastern Europe for the purchase of food during the holidays, for a total outlay of almost $1.2 million in direct support of rescuers."[21]

A few noteworthy exceptions aside,[22] this relatively late but truly dedicated support in Israel and the United States for the rescuers themselves predates most of the significant but limited literature about the rescuers. It was perhaps the very dearth of help given to the Jews by non-Jews in Nazi-dominated Europe that recently created interest in the moral courage of those relative few who stood by the Jews in their greatest time of need. After all, as Cynthia Ozick points out, the rescuers do not constitute a category that can be measured by number, "its measure is metaphysical, and belongs to the sublime."[23] In the 1990s, more people were willing to speak and to hear about the rescuers. Abraham Foxman, who was saved by his nanny in Vilna, spoke about this transition at the Hidden Child Conference in Jerusalem in July 1993: "For the first fifty years after the Holocaust, survivors bore witness to evil, brutality, and bestiality. Now is the time for us, for our generation, to bear witness to goodness. For each one of us is living proof that even in hell, even in that hell called the Holocaust, there was goodness, there was kindness, and there was love and compassion."[24]

Simultaneously, a limited literature about the rescuers began

20. See the newly reconstituted Web site of the Jewish Foundation for the Righteous (www.jfr.org) for additional information.

21. E-mail to author from Jonathan Gruber of the JFR, December 21, 2004.

22. Naturally, I am thinking of the major contributions made by Philip Hallie, *Lest Innocent Blood Be Shed* (1979); Pierre Sauvage, *Weapons of the Spirit* (1987); Carol Rittner and Sondra Myers, eds., *The Courage to Care* (1986); Nechama Tec, *When Light Pierced the Darkness* (1986); and Samuel P. Oliner and Pearl M. Oliner, *The Altruistic Personality: Rescuers of Jews in Nazi Europe* (New York: The Free Press, 1988).

23. Cynthia Ozick, "Prologue," in Block and Drucker, *Rescuers*, xiv.

24. Gilbert, *The Righteous*, xvii.

to appear in the mid-1990s,[25] but still today, literature about rescue is relatively scarce and most general books on the Holocaust do not have chapters on the rescuers. Much work remains to be done. "As recently as 1991," writes Eva Fogelman, "when Mishi Harmon, an eight-year-old Israeli boy, wanted to research the life of [Raoul] Wallenberg for a school project, he found there was not one book in Hebrew on Wallenberg."[26] In 1994, Rabbi Schulweis lamented: "How ironic that our children and we ourselves know the names of Klaus Barbie, Goebbels, Goering, Eichmann, Himmler, and Hitler but not the names of those who risked their lives to hide and protect the Frank family. Are not the names of Victor Kugler and Jan Kleinman and Miep Giess and Elizabeth Van Vosquijl to be remembered in remembering the Holocaust?"[27] Closer to home, how many Americans know that, until 2006, we had only one "Righteous Gentile"? A man who left for Marseille on August 15, 1940, with plans to stay for a month, $3,000 taped to his leg, and a list of two hundred Jewish intellectuals and artists he hoped to save. He stayed for thirteen months, fighting both Vichy and the U.S. State Department at every turn, until he was finally expelled from France. But, by that time, he had saved more than two thousand refugees, including Marcel Duchamp, Marc Chagall, Jacques Lipchitz, Max Ernst, Max

25. A list of major contributions to the literature of rescue published since 1990 would include: Gay Block and Malka Drucker, *Portraits of Moral Courage in the Holocaust* (1992); Eva Fogelman, *Conscience and Courage: Rescuers of Jews During the Holocaust* (1994); Martin Gilbert, *The Righteous: The Unsung Heroes of the Holocaust* (2003); Mordecai Paldiel, *Saving the Jews: Amazing Stories of Men and Women Who Defied the "Final Solution"* (2000); Lucien Lazare, *Rescue as Resistance: How Jewish Organizations Fought the Holocaust in France* (1996); Pierre Bolle et al., eds., *Le Plateau Vivarais-Lignon: Accueil et Résistance 1939–1944* (1992); David R. Blumenthal, *The Banality of Good and Evil: Moral Lessons from the Shoah and Jewish Tradition* (1999); David P. Gushee, *The Righteous Gentiles of the Holocaust: A Christian Interpretation* (Minneapolis, Minn.: Fortress Press, 1994); Kristen Renwick Monroe, *The Heart of Altruism: Perceptions of a Common Humanity* (Princeton, N.J.: Princeton University Press, 1996) and *The Hand of Compassion: Portraits of Moral Choice during the Holocaust* (Princeton, N.J.: Princeton University Press, 2004).
26. Fogelman, *Conscience and Courage*, 303–4.
27. Schulweis, *For Those Who Can't Believe*, 153.

Ophüls, Arthur Koestler, Hannah Arendt, and André Breton. How many Americans have ever heard the name Varian Fry, our national hero who died in obscurity?[28]

⌣⟶

Finding *the* motivating factor for rescuers is even more difficult than ascertaining how many rescuers there were. There simply was no single motivating factor among rescuers of Jews during the Holocaust that can account for this courageous altruism. As with collaboration, rescue had a thousand faces. Many of the researchers of this question, however, have found clusters of motivating factors that appear frequently in the rescuers they have interviewed. Nechama Tec, whose pioneering work *When Light Pierced The Darkness: Christian Rescue of Jews in Nazi-Occupied Poland* ranks among the first major studies of rescue, is a Holocaust survivor whose family was hidden by Poles "whose main motivation was money."[29] In her attempt to fathom the reasons why Poles risked their lives and those of their family members to save Jews, she interviewed sixty-five people (thirty-four Jews and thirty-one non-Jewish Poles) in Poland, Israel, Canada, and the United States. Each interview lasted between two and eight hours. She also collected data from a variety of other sources. In sum, she collected evidence from 189 Poles and 308 Jews, with the Jewish survivors providing "adequate descriptions [of] about 565 Polish helpers."[30] Tec discovered a handful of characteristics that most, but not all, rescuers shared. The most important of these characteristics are "the tradition of standing up for the needy" and "individuality" or marginality (separate-

28. Sheila Isenberg's study, *A Hero of Our Own: The Story of Varian Fry* (New York: Random House, 2001), is the first biography of Fry to appear in any language.

29. Tec, *When Light Pierced The Darkness*, viii. In compiling her views on rescuer motivation, I have tapped three sources: the book just cited, 184–93; "Helping Behavior and Rescue during the Holocaust," in *Lessons and Legacies: The Meaning of the Holocaust in a Changing World*, ed. Peter Hayes (Evanston, Ill.: Northwestern University Press, 1991), 210–24; and her entry "Righteous Among the Nations" in *The Holocaust Encyclopedia*, 569–74.

30. Tec, *When Light Pierced The Darkness*, 205.

ness from their social environment). The rest of the characteristics that "tend to follow from these two basic factors" include: "independence or self-reliance to act in accordance with personal convictions, regardless of how these are viewed by others" and "universalistic perceptions of Jews that defined them as helpless beings . . . totally dependent on the protection of others." Here too, Tec notes the rescuers' ability to disregard all attributes "except those that expressed extreme suffering and need" and the fact that their values had been incorporated into their moral constitution well before the war began.[31] Six years after Tec published these findings, Gay Block and Malka Drucker, who interviewed 105 rescuers from eleven different countries, published *Rescuers: Portraits of Moral Courage in the Holocaust,* in which they confirm that the rescuers they interviewed "supported the findings of Nechama Tec's personality profile."[32]

In 1988, two years after Tec's study, Samuel P. and Pearl M. Oliner published what is generally considered one of the most encompassing analyses of rescuer motivation during the Holocaust. In *The Altruistic Personality: Rescuers of Jews in Nazi Europe,* the Oliners, who interviewed 406 rescuers, 126 nonrescuers, and 150 survivors, developed a "composite portrait" of the typical rescuer that also stresses individuality, independence, dependability, self-reliance, and the tradition of standing up for the needy. Rather than autonomy, the Oliners emphasize the rescuers' "capacity for extensive relationships—their stronger sense of attachment to others and their feeling of responsibility for the welfare of others, including those outside their immediate familial or communal circles." In addition, the Oliners underscore "close family relationships in which parents model caring behavior and communicate caring values" in homes where "parental discipline tends toward leniency . . .

31. Ibid., 191, 188, 189. Fifteen years later, when Tec compares the motivations of rescuers from several European countries, the characteristics are basically the same as those she had found earlier among the Poles. See Nechama Tec, "Righteous Among the Nations," in *The Holocaust Encyclopedia,* 574.

32. Block and Drucker, *Rescuers,* 1, 5–6, 9.

[and] physical punishment is rare," and parents who set high standards for their children, "particularly with regard to caring for others," discipline them "with a heavy dose of reasoning," and rather than insisting on obedience, explain "why behaviors are inappropriate, often with reference to their consequences for others."[33]

For her masterful and original study *Conscience and Courage: Rescuers of Jews During the Holocaust* (1994), Eva Fogelman interviewed over three hundred rescuers. She divides the rescuers into five distinct categories (moral, Judeophilic, network, concerned professionalism, children) and finds that, in general, rescue was "the expression of the values and beliefs of a person . . . nurtured in childhood that came to expression during the Holocaust . . . and continued in the postwar years." Most of her rescuers were asked to help and whether they did so depended on a combination of character and situational considerations. The rescuers were not suicidal. They rescued others when they felt they had "a very good chance of succeeding. . . . The circumstances, timing, and opportunity for rescue had to be just right." Far more important than the circumstances, however, were the following factors, and while not all rescuers experienced one or more of them, Fogelman insists that a majority of rescuers did: "A nurturing, loving home; an altruistic parent or beloved caretaker who served as a role model for altruistic behavior; a tolerance for people who were different; a childhood illness or personal loss that tested their resilience and exposed them to special care; and an upbringing that emphasized independence, competence, discipline with explanations (rather than physical punishment or withdrawal of love), and caring."[34]

Finally, in *The Heart of Altruism: Perceptions of a Common Humanity* and *The Hand of Compassion: Portraits of Moral Choice during the Holocaust*, Kristen Monroe studies altruism in general and more specifically the pure altruism demonstrated by the rescuers of Jews

33. Oliner and Oliner, *The Altruistic Personality*, 249, 249–50.
34. Fogelman, *Conscience and Courage*, xviii; 59; 254.

during the Holocaust. Monroe argues that altruism can never be fully comprehended when viewed "within the paradigmatic confines of self-interest."[35] This is certainly one of the major contributions of her illuminating work. More specifically, with regard to the rescuers, Monroe agrees with Tec, the Oliners, and Fogelman that "a wide variety of forces influenced rescuers; no single factor can be said to have caused their rescue behavior . . . The driving force behind moral action thus seems both complex and multidimensional."[36] But Monroe affirms that all rescuers had a sense of shared humanity. "It was the common factor among all the altruists I interviewed, the only one that refused to go away under the most careful scrutiny . . . [It was] a very simple but deeply felt recognition that we all share certain characteristics and are entitled to certain rights, merely by virtue of our common humanity." This recognition of a common humanity was activated by any number of factors "from genetic coding and religious teachings to group or kinship ties and psychic utility."[37] Altruists have different starting points in reaching the same end. Monroe insists that it is not the rescuers' sense of self that is the key here but the rescuers' sense of self in relation to their sense of others. At the broadest theoretical level, Monroe develops a theory of ethical political action predicated neither on reason nor religion but on identity, which supersedes consciously held moral values that themselves evolve from one's "core identity."[38]

Rescue is basically a function of character and core values but it also depends upon environmental circumstances. Many people, for example, wanted to help but did not have the material resources to do so. Others who also would have been willing to become involved in rescue were not situated in a place where they would have had any chance of being successful in doing so. This is why Eva Fo-

---

35. Monroe, *The Heart of Altruism*, 197.
36. Monroe, *The Hand of Compassion*, 187.
37. Monroe, *The Heart of Altruism*, 206; 214.
38. Ibid. In this regard, see also 217–32.

gelman maintains that "a personality test can never accurately predict who will or will not become a rescuer. Action may come from the core of the self, but it is inhibited or reinforced by situational factors."[39] As a result, we can be far more certain about what did *not* matter regarding rescuer motivation than what did. In this vein, on the whole, gender, age, nationality, ethnicity, level of education, profession, economic status, religious leaning, political persuasion, family size, social status, birth order within the family, belief in an afterlife, hatred of the Nazis did not play a determining role as to who would become a rescuer. The rescuers are remarkably diverse and come from all segments of society.

Examining religion as a possible motivating factor, for example, demonstrates the thorny nature of the task at hand. Religion often fosters respect for human life but at the same time it places people into exclusive groups that historically have been antagonistic to one another. It would be difficult to claim that religion mattered during the Holocaust when 99.5 percent of baptized Christians did nothing to help Jews. But what about those persons who did rescue Jews? How many maintained that religion was a motivating force in their acts of rescue? The answer is, perhaps surprisingly, not very many. In Poland, for example, the Catholic Church was traditionally anti-Semitic and had no uniform wartime policy regarding the Jews. Without a papal decree or a national Catholic stance, individuals within the clergy and laity alike were on their own regarding the rescue of Jews. Nechama Tec found that, among Polish rescuers, "only 27 percent attributed their help to Jews to religious convictions." Since almost all of these persons were baptized Catholics and most of them devout practicing Christians, this certainly downplays the importance of religion as a motive of rescue even in the most fervent Catholic country in Europe. By contrast, 95 percent of these same Polish rescuers claim to have acted out of

39. Fogelman, *Conscience and Courage*, 66.

"compassion for Jewish suffering." The Oliners, who interviewed rescuers from all over Europe, note that "religion, God, or Christianity was cited by 15 percent of rescuers," and Fogelman, who identifies a group of "religious-moral rescuers [who] described their sense of right and wrong in religious rather than ethical terms," remarks that such persons constituted only 12 percent of the rescuers she interviewed.[40] Religion was not therefore a determining factor for the great majority of rescuers. David Gushee concludes that "a surprisingly low percentage of rescuers cite religion as even one of their motivations."[41]

Nonetheless, a very small minority of Christian rescuers did rescue out of a sense of Christian duty. Why did they do so when most Christians did nothing to help Jews and the great majority of Christians who did risk their lives to save Jews did so for other reasons? In *The Righteous Gentiles of the Holocaust: A Christian Interpretation*, David Gushee gives six basic reasons why these Christians rescued for religious motives. Three of these reasons—the incompatibility of Nazism and Christian faith, the equality and preciousness of every human life, the Biblical teachings on compassion and love—do not seem definitive because they should have been obvious to all Christians. The others are more specific to the issue: the tradition of Christian pacifism (André Trocmé and Edouard Theis in Le Chambon-sur-Lignon); a strong sense of religious kinship with Jews as a people (valid for the Lutheran Church of Denmark and in particular the French Huguenots and the Dutch Reform Church, both of which were influenced by Calvin's philo-Semitism); and the remembered experience of religious persecution (by French Huguenots and a Baptist minority in Lithuania and Western Ukraine). Gushee underscores the fact that "most of these devout Christian rescuers

40. Tec, *When Light Pierced the Darkness*, 145; Oliner and Oliner, *The Altruistic Personality*, 155; Fogelman, *Conscience and Courage*, 163. For the percentage in Fogelman, see Gushee, *The Righteous Gentiles of the Holocaust*, 112.
41. Gushee, *The Righteous Gentiles of the Holocaust*, 112.

were people deeply rooted in a particular historic faith community"[42] (Dutch Reformed, French Darbyites, Italian Catholics, Ukrainian Baptists, French Huguenots, and German Lutherans).

Lawrence Baron's work on the Dutch Calvinists supports Gushee's findings. Baron notes that the Dutch Calvinists rescued Jews "primarily for theological reasons" and he cites rescuers who claim that "Christians had an obligation to save God's chosen people."[43] Religion is also an important motivation given by many rescuers on the plateau Vivarais-Lignon. But there is no truth to Tzvetan Todorov's claim that "the Darbyite sect (Protestant fundamentalists) also present in the region [along with the Reformed Protestant majority] practiced a different solidarity: They preferred to save Jews, rather than other French people, for example, because they saw in them 'the people of the Book.'"[44] Todorov may be thinking of the testimony given by Mme Brottes in Pierre Sauvage's powerful documentary *Weapons of the Spirit*. Mme Brottes says: ". . . they were the people of God. That is what mattered." But it is equally important to remember that about fifteen hundred of the five thousand refugees hidden on the plateau were not Jewish. The tradition of hospitality and refuge in the area was available to all persons regardless of ethnic origin, religion, or nationality.

In the final analysis, the motivating factors for the rescue of Jews in Europe during the Holocaust reinforce one another, but all rescuers do not reflect one pattern and all nonrescuers another. The traits commonly found among the rescuers were neither necessary nor sufficient. Some people who did not have those traits rescued Jews while others who did have them failed to rescue persecuted people. Nevertheless, the following traits are commonly

42. Ibid., 147, 117–48.

43. Lawrence Baron, "The Dutchness of Dutch Rescuers: The National Dimension of Altruism," in *Embracing the Other: Philosophical, Psychological, and Historical Perspectives,* ed. Pearl Oliner et al. (New York: New York University Press, 1992), 317, 318, 320.

44. Tzvetan Todorov, *Face à l'extrême* (Paris: Editions du Seuil, 1991), 93.

found in the majority of interviewed rescuers: a nurturing, loving home where children are taught caring values, altruistic parents or a caretaker as a role model for altruistic behavior, tolerance for people who are different, independence, self-reliance, self-confidence, moderate self-esteem, a history of giving aid to the needy, a belief in a common humanity, and the ability to act according to one's own values regardless of what others do. Most important, Eva Fogelman notes that 89 percent of the rescuers she interviewed "had a parent or adult figure who acted as an altruistic role model."[45] This factor plays heavily too in the Oliners' study, but they warn us that "to suggest that all rescuers developed altruistic and inclusive inclinations because of good family relationships oversimplifies the complex realities."[46] Kristen Monroe concludes: "For the most part, altruists had, in fact, been instilled with high ethical standards by a critical role model. But this was not uniformly so."[47] This "for the most part" in all these studies is important. Regarding rescuer motivation, there is no "uniformly so," no "in all cases."

The belief in a common humanity is expressed differently in each of these studies. Nechama Tec speaks of "universalistic principles," meaning that the rescuers offered help to anyone in need and did not see the Jews as Jews "but only as haunted, persecuted human beings in desperate need of aid."[48] The influence of these universalistic principles is confirmed by the fact that some Poles rescued individual Jews whom they neither liked nor respected, and by the fact that "only nine percent of these [interviewed] rescuers limited their help to friends."[49] The Oliners express this "consistently universalistic orientation" in terms of "inclusiveness" and "extensivity": "For most rescuers, helping Jews was an expression of

45. Fogelman, *Conscience and Courage*, 263.
46. Oliner and Oliner, *The Altruistic Personality*, 183.
47. Monroe, *The Heart of Altruism*, 184.
48. Tec, *When Light Pierced the Darkness*, 189.
49. On the first point, see *When Light Pierced the Darkness*, 189; on the second, Nechama Tec, "Helping Behavior and Rescue during the Holocaust," 223.

ethical principles that extended to all of humanity." They write that "knowing only whether someone was characterized by an extensive or a constricted orientation enabled us to predict who would be a rescuer or a nonrescuer for 70 percent of the individuals we studied."[50] Eva Fogelman cites the Oliners' findings and subscribes to their "democratic principle 'inclusiveness,'"[51] while Kristen Monroe maintains that all rescuers saw themselves "as bound to all mankind through a common humanity."[52] "For rescuers," she writes, "the morally salient category was the human race, not ethnicity, religion, or political affiliation."[53] But what about that small exceptional group of anti-Semites who rescued Jews? Did they "identify" with Jews? Or did they help them for other reasons without identifying with them? According to Nechama Tec, most of these anti-Semite rescuers were devout Catholics who had a history of helping the needy. Most of them remained anti-Semites after the war. Undoubtedly they believed in a common humanity in the sense that help should be offered to all persons in desperate need, but it is certainly not clear that these anti-Semite rescuers defined themselves or identified themselves in relation to *all* others. As one survivor explained to Tec: "It is one thing to help an underdog and quite another to consider him as an equal."[54]

Regarding the supposed social marginality of rescuers, the findings of most studies differ from those of Nechama Tec, who concludes that "with only a few exceptions, but in different ways and in different degrees, the Poles in my study did not fit into their milieux."[55] Eva Fogelman, for example, maintains that ". . . before the war [the rescuers] had been very much part of their communities," and the Oliners claim that "the overwhelming majority of rescuers

50. Oliner and Oliner, *The Altruistic Personality*, 166, 170, 253.
51. Fogelman, *Conscience and Courage*, 262.
52. Monroe, *The Heart of Altruism*, 5.
53. Monroe, *The Hand of Compassion*, 234.
54. Tec, *When Light Pierced the Darkness*, 106; and more generally 99–109.
55. Ibid., 188.

(80 percent) had a sense of belonging to their community."[56] Lawrence Baron, whose research centers on Dutch rescuers, explains this discrepancy by noting that marginality was more evident in Poland, where anti-Semitism was very strong and most Jews unassimilated, than in Holland, Denmark, Italy, and even France:

> It is telling that so few of the Dutch rescuers can be classified as socially marginal like the Polish rescuers in Nechama Tec's sample. Since positive attitudes towards Jews represented a prewar consensus in Dutch public opinion, the rescuers of Jews stemmed more from the mainstream of Dutch society than from its margins. Their aid to the Jews represented a normative altruism in keeping with typical Dutch values and was akin to the sort of altruism exhibited by the Danes and the Italians.[57]

Fogelman and the Oliners stress the fact that rescuers were disciplined by explanation "rather than physical punishment or withdrawal of love."[58] But in analyzing this aspect of the Oliners' study, David Gushee points out that only 21 percent of the rescuers reported this way of having been disciplined. This is proportionately significant when compared to the 6 percent of nonrescuers who reported this same method of childhood discipline in their lives, but it nonetheless indicates that 79 percent of the rescuers never mention it.[59] Obedience *per se* was not stressed in the homes of future rescuers (only 1 percent of the rescuers in the Oliners' study, for example, claim that their parents emphasized obedience as compared to 9 percent of nonrescuers and 12 percent of bystanders).[60] In almost all cases one had to disobey to rescue persecuted people. There were, however, several people in and around Le Chambon-sur-

56. Fogelman, *Conscience and Courage*, 67; Oliner and Oliner, *The Altruistic Personality*, 176.

57. Lawrence Baron, "The Dutchness of Dutch Rescuers," 322.

58. Fogelman, *Conscience and Courage*, 254.

59. Oliner and Oliner, *The Altruistic Personality*, 181–82; Gushee, *The Righteous Gentiles of the Holocaust*, 96.

60. Oliner and Oliner, *The Altruistic Personality*, 162.

Lignon who, when asked why they hid Jewish people on their farms and in their homes, responded "because Pastor Trocmé asked me to." Finally, there is the intriguing but minor factor mentioned only by Fogelman, that "a childhood illness or personal loss" was significant among rescuers. Fogelman found that such persons were cared for with love during their trauma and thus developed a special sensitivity to the suffering of others.[61]

The rescuers were ordinary people who, when asked for help, as were two-thirds of the rescuers interviewed by the Oliners,[62] responded with courage and generosity. They did so almost instinctively. This was in part because, as all the major studies indicate, the great majority of rescuers had already developed an altruistic personality before the Nazi campaign against the Jews began. Given that millions of nonrescuers must also have had altruistic personalities, it is important to underscore, as Leonard Grob does in his probing existential reading of the phenomenon of rescue in Nazi-dominated Europe, that the values of the rescuers had to be activated in real time by each individual.[63] Nonetheless all the major studies show that the responses of the majority of rescuers were spontaneous, as though there were no other course of action available to them. Helping the needy had become habitual in their lives. As one of the rescuers, Otto Springer, told Kristen Monroe: "The hand of compassion was faster than the calculus of reason."[64] Magda Trocmé is equally illuminating on this question:

> Those of us who received the first Jews did what we thought had to be done—nothing more complicated. It was not decided from one day to the next what we would have to do. There were many people in the village who needed help. How could we refuse them? A person doesn't sit down and say I'm going to do this and this and that.

61. Fogelman, *Conscience and Courage*, 254, 268–70.
62. Oliner and Oliner, *The Altruistic Personality*, 132–41.
63. Leonard Grob, "Rescue during the Holocaust—and Today," *Judaism* 46 (1997): 98–107.
64. Monroe, *The Hand of Compassion*, v.

We had no time to think. When a problem came, we had to solve it immediately. Sometimes people ask me, "How did you make a decision?" There was no decision to make. The issue was: Do you think we are all brothers or not? Do you think it is unjust to turn in the Jews or not? Then let us try to help.[65]

Yet all these studies and interviews with the rescuers cannot explain everything about the rescue of Jews during the Holocaust. There is something mysterious about the rescuers that escapes our facts, figures, examples, and percentages. Try as we might, they always elude our grasp whenever we attempt to seize them collectively. This mystery of goodness is uplifting. The rescuers embody the moral potential that makes us proud to be human beings. But when we look at the people of Europe as a whole from 1933 to 1945, the mystery of why and how so few cared about the fate of so many darkens the horizon.

There are no positive lessons emerging from the Holocaust. There are several negative ones: (1) not only could the Holocaust happen again, next time it will be easier; (2) if someone tells you that the inconceivable is happening, it may very well be true; (3) just because something has not already happened does not mean that it is not taking place. Berel Lang calls these "certain practical cautions." He strikingly identifies two others: "*Do* believe what you see, even if you can't imagine it"; and ". . . there is *no* 'here' of which one can say with assurance, 'It can't happen here.'"[66] The Holocaust was not unique (a one-time occurrence). One speaks today rather of the "unprecedented nature" of the Holocaust in general or of its "unprecedented features" that occurred for the first time during the Holocaust but can happen again.[67]

65. Carol Rittner and Sondra Myers, eds., *The Courage to Care*, 102.
66. Berel Lang, *The Future of the Holocaust: Between History and Memory* (Ithaca, N.Y.: Cornell University Press, 1999), 178–81.
67. I have found two such discussions particularly fruitful: Lang, *The Future of the Holocaust*, 77–91; Yehuda Bauer, *Rethinking the Holocaust*, passim.

Do the rescuers teach us anything positive with regard to our present and future? The answer of those who have written extensively about the rescuers is an overwhelming "Yes." These same authors insist that, as post-Holocaust people, we have a moral obligation to apply these "lessons" to our present-day reality. Even among those Holocaust scholars who have not written extensively about the rescuers, we find the admonition to spread whatever of value can be gleaned from their courageous behavior. Yehuda Bauer, for example, observes that "the existence of rescuers on the margins provides a hope that these evils are not inevitable, that they can be fought." He concludes that "the Holocaust is a warning. It adds three commandments to the ten of the Jewish-Christian tradition: *Thou shalt not be a perpetrator; Thou shalt not be a passive victim;* and *Thou most certainly shalt not be a bystander.* We do not know whether we will succeed in spreading this knowledge. But if there is even a chance in a million that sense should prevail, we have a moral obligation, in the spirit of Kantian moral philosophy, to try."[68] Even among those who do not believe that teaching the Holocaust can prevent future genocides or who doubt that any positive lessons can be extracted from the Holocaust, there is still sometimes mention of the importance of the rescuers in teaching morality. Stanley Kauffman, reviewing Aviva Slesin's documentary *Secret Lives: Hidden Children and Their Rescuers During World War II,* remarks: "It is precisely because the memory of the Holocaust will not—does not—prevent further programmed killings that such a film is welcome. It lets us glimpse once again the stubborn, if slender, persistence of the humane."[69] Peter Novick doubts that anything redemptive or useful can be drawn from the Holocaust. Even so, he notes that "it can't hurt to try" to "inculcate values or moral/political lessons" in schools and "if curricula on the Holocaust are a convenient

68. Yehuda Bauer, *Rethinking the Holocaust,* xi, 67.
69. Stanley Kauffmann, "A Bouquet of Lives," *The New Republic,* June 9, 2003, 24.

framework, why not?"[70] Without deforming the event, these critics imply, we must try to ascertain what can be learned from it.

Among those who have written extensively on the rescuers, the claims for relevance are explicit and compelling. They urge us to teach their findings and not to forget those few who remembered the Jews during the Nazi plague. Rabbi Harold Schulweis insists on the teaching of the rescuers so that "the evidence of goodness [will] not be buried in anonymity or lost in a footnote or damned with faint praise," which would "help twist history into a metaphysical fatalism that ordains anti-Semitism as an eternal recurrence" and hide the fact that "there was and always are alternatives to passive complicity with cruel powers."[71] Since the rescuers "represent the highest form of moral achievement," Malka Drucker says, they can "teach us about courage and compassion . . . and altruism."[72] Nechama Tec concludes that studying the Holocaust "can have lessons and legacies beyond the particular time, place, events, and people."[73] She underscores the fact that the reality of the rescuers "denies the inevitable supremacy of evil . . . With this denial comes hope."[74]

Because our generation was not called upon to rescue Jews during the Holocaust but to restructure the world after Auschwitz, the question to which we must respond is not the excruciatingly unanswerable "What would I have done had I lived in Occupied Europe?" but the much more urgently concrete "What can we do now to help build a world where another Auschwitz would be unthinkable?" We do have a model to work with—the rescuers of Jews during the Holocaust. David Gushee, writing from a deeply Christian tradition, underscores the fact that there were numerous paths that led to the moral goodness of the rescuers who "challenge each of us to con-

70. Peter Novick, *The Holocaust in American Life*, 263, 260.
71. Schulweis, *For Those Who Can't Believe*, 153, 154, 156.
72. Block and Drucker, *Rescuers*, 10, 1.
73. Tec, "Helping Behavior and Rescue During the Holocaust," 224.
74. Tec, *When Light Pierced the Darkness*, 5.

sider whether we are journeying along even one of these paths."[75] Leonard Grob, writing from the Jewish tradition of *Tikkun Olam* ("mending the world"), observes that the rescuers provide us "with a model of resistance to indifference and indecision." He urges us to see that "we can, and must, open a clearing within which our young people can envision themselves as doers of good."[76] Samuel and Pearl Oliner emphasize the importance of "extensivity" in the rescuers they interviewed and recommend that "schools . . . become institutions that not only prepare students for academic competence but also help them to acquire an extensive orientation to others." The rescuers made a choice, the Oliners conclude, "that affirmed the value and meaningfulness of each life in the midst of a diabolical social order that repeatedly denied it. Can we do otherwise?"[77] Finally, Eva Fogelman admits that the most important question lying at the heart of her research project is whether or not the moral courage of the rescuers can be taught. She concludes that an understanding of what motivated the rescuers can provide a model for mobilizing social action in our own communities: "Government, religious and social institutions need to create programs in which people can channel their altruistic energies . . . With more imaginative encouragement, people could become what Robert Lifton has called 'species selves,' people who can reach beyond their own nationality and race and embrace others."[78]

Five points, above all, need to be stressed in teaching the rescuers. First, although much altruism can indeed be explained in terms of self-interest, the pure life-threatening altruism of the rescuers cannot be explained in such terms. The punishments for hiding Jewish people during the Holocaust ranged from concentration camps, to death, to the murder of one's entire family, and the great

75. Gushee, *The Righteous Gentiles of the Holocaust*, 116.

76. Leonard Grob, "Rescue During the Holocaust—and Today," 106, 104.

77. Oliner and Oliner, *The Altruistic Personality*, 258, 260.

78. Fogelman, *Conscience and Courage*, xv, 322. R. J. Lifton, *The Future of Immortality and Other Essays for a Nuclear Age* (New York: Basic Books, 1987), 111–12, 133–35.

majority of rescuers risked their lives to save strangers. Eva Fogelman, a psychiatrist herself, corrects psychiatry's traditional "negative" view of such altruists:

> Beyond a personal mission to record individual instances of moral
> courage during an immoral time, my book has a broader goal, I want
> to give altruism back its good name. It is not a concept with which
> people are very comfortable or about which they know very much.
> Altruistically inclined people are seen as weaklings, as "do-gooders."
> Psychoanalysts dismiss the act of rescue as narcissism overlaid with
> rescue fantasies, or they assign it unconscious defenses such as the
> need for power or the need to be loved. Holocaust scholars relegate
> rescuers' deeds to a footnote.[79]

While unconscious motivations surely played a role in inducing individuals to rescue, "intangibles such as personal gratification and
enhanced self-image were small rewards indeed for the vast risks
these people undertook."[80]

Michael Bader also notes that neither traditional Freudian psychoanalysts nor modern progressive psychoanalysts consider "a
wish to improve the welfare of the other as a primary human striv-
ing."[81] Even when altruism is recognized, it is systematically sub-
ordinated to other impulses and is consistently discredited as a
foundational motivation. But the rescuers exhibit the presence of
primary altruism. Because human beings performed these acts of

79. Fogelman, *Conscience and Courage*, xix.
80. Ibid., 158.
81. Michael Bader, "Looking a Gift Horse in the Mouth," *Tikkun* (Sept.–Oct.
1998): 13–14. Recognizing the importance of the rescuers also coheres with *Tikkun*'s
view of the appropriate legacy of the Holocaust, which is the necessity of the "moral
reawakening or ethical purification of the world" rather than the idea that survival is
"the topmost value and purpose of life," or, as Peter Gabel words it, the struggle of
being "to know itself as Love that realizes itself through the affirmation of the other, through the I-Thou relation." See respectively: Zygmunt Bauman, "The Holocaust's
Life as a Ghost," *Tikkun* (July–August 1998): 36, 34; Peter Gabel, "The Meaning of the
Holocaust: Social Alienation and the Infliction of Human Suffering," *Tikkun* (Nov.–
Dec. 1998): 13.

moral courage, human beings are capable of performing such acts of moral courage. Primary altruistic tendencies coexist with those of self-interest. The view that both egoism and altruism are natural tendencies is supported not only by psychiatrists such as Fogelman and Bader; some biologists also claim that "humans evolved to be altruistic because groups in which members help each other fare better than those in which each member stands alone."[82] If we wish to form individuals who resemble the rescuers and communities that will produce such individuals, we will have to emphasize altruism as a foundational motivation of human behavior. Today's general view that traditionally conceived narrow self-interest is at the heart of all human activity is the greatest tool for the maintenance of the status quo and the ultimate justification of bystander behavior. The actions of the rescuers of Jews during the Holocaust enable us to recognize the possibility of liberating ourselves from narrow self-interest, and of acknowledging that concern for the other is a natural motivation of human behavior.

It is also important to emphasize that, however multidimensional the phenomenon of rescue may have been, most rescuers had already developed altruistic personalities before the Holocaust began. Lawrence Baron points out that Oskar Schindler was the exception and that it is a serious mistake to conclude from his biography that "there must be little continuity between one's normal ethics and one's reaction to crises such as Jewish suffering in the Holocaust."[83] Quite to the contrary, all the major writers on the rescuers reach the same conclusion: rather than aberrant behavior caused by the horrors of World War II, rescue activity normally grew out of core values practiced over a lifetime by self-reliant and self-confident persons who had a habit of standing up for the needy.

82. Annie Murphy Paul, "Born to be Good?" *USA Weekend*, July 23–25, 1999, 6.

83. Lawrence Baron, "Teaching about the New Psychosocial Research on Rescuers in Holocaust Courses," in *Lessons and Legacies II: Teaching the Holocaust in a Changing World*, ed. Donald G. Schilling (Evanston, Ill.: Northwestern University Press, 1998), 133.

This explains in large measure why so many of the rescuers felt that what they did hardly warranted attention, much less praise. It seemed ordinary to them, for it was their normal way of relating to others. They simply continued to act humanely at a time when to do so could have cost them their life. *What* they did (feed hungry people, give a bed or a barn to someone to sleep in, hide an innocent person from a violent enemy) was simply decent, not heroic. But *when* they did what they did rendered their actions extraordinary.

Third, it is essential to stress that most rescuers developed altruistic personalities because they had parents or caretakers who taught them to care for the needy. It is equally important to understand that these parents and caretakers taught by example. In *Face à l'extrême*, Tzvetan Todorov makes the significant point that compassion is not normally a virtue of either children or adolescents, who tend to "discover justice well before mercy."[84] Even if one were to argue that compassion is a natural instinct, it would be so in the sense that a beard is natural to men. Natural but not evident for some time. Therefore it must form a part of each child's education. All the more so if one agrees with Cynthia Ozick, who writes, "I do not—cannot—believe that human beings are, without explicit teaching, naturally or intrinsically altruistic."[85] In any event, since example is primordial in the education of children, compassion must be exhibited by each child's role models. This truth is brought out repeatedly in Robert Coles's *The Moral Intelligence of Children*: "the most persuasive moral teaching we adults do is by example: The witness of our lives."[86] To those who ask, "Can compassion be taught?" there is the affirmative testimony of the majority of the interviewed rescuers of Jews during the Holocaust that it can be taught by example.

It is also necessary to point out that the altruism of the rescu-

84. Tzvetan Todorov, *Face à l'extrême*, 326–27.
85. Cynthia Ozick, "Prologue," in Block and Drucker, *Rescuers*, xvi.
86. Robert Coles, *The Moral Intelligence of Children* (New York: Random House, 1997), 31.

ers was in very large measure an altruism extended universally. The great majority of rescuers, free of any sense whatsoever of "us" and "them," helped the needy regardless of their ethnic origins or religion. Finally, it is vital to focus on issues of similarity and difference. At the time of their courageous actions, Hitler was preaching a doctrine of radical, racial difference between human beings. The official handbook of the Hitler Youth organization, for example, states: "The foundation of the National Socialist outlook on life is the perception of the unlikeness of men."[87] Aryans headed the list on which the Jews were at the bottom. The rescuers were open to people judged to be "different," precisely because they saw them as the same. What drove the great majority of rescuers was the belief that the Jews were in fact just like everybody else. This is why what was happening to them was, for the rescuers, completely unacceptable. The great majority of the rescuers were not celebrating diversity when they hid Jewish people in their barns. On the contrary, confronted with a vicious doctrine of racial hatred, at the risk of their lives they affirmed the fundamental similarity of all human beings. This is what André Trocmé meant when, on August 10, 1942, he told the Vichy official who asked him to turn over the Jews hiding in the village: "We don't know what a Jew is. We only know men."

The behavior of the rescuers shows that in a world obsessed with difference, one can make a difference only by insisting on the essential similarity between all human beings. This is not tantamount, however, to negating differences which are real and must be recognized and respected. The truth revealed in the accounts of the rescuers is that differences exist at the cultural level, but at the human level there are no fundamental differences between human beings. Montaigne establishes an equilibrium between similarity and difference: "If our faces were not similar," he writes, "we could not distinguish man from beast; if they were not dissimilar, we could not

87. Philip Hallie, *Lest Innocent Blood Be Shed*, 273.

distinguish man from man."[88] Genocide occurs when the balance is shattered and one can see only the difference of others. In his chapter on "useless violence" in *The Drowned and the Saved*, Primo Levi asks why the Nazis didn't just kill the Jews immediately. Why did they drag it out? Why did they deport Jewish people who were dying in hospitals in their native countries? Why the gratuitous viciousness and senseless, cruel humiliations, treating humans as cattle, leaving them, for example, in packed railroad wagons for two weeks (as was the case with Jews deported from Salonika) without a latrine or something to function as one? The sole usefulness that Levi could find in this "useless violence," which degraded the victims and made many of them act despicably, was that they would then appear different, less human, and as a result, it would be easier for the murderers to kill them. As Stangl, "that most diligent Treblinka henchman," explained, it would be easier for "the material executors of the operations . . . to do what they were doing." Levi concludes that "before dying the victim must be degraded, so that the murderer will be less burdened by guilt."[89]

Berel Lang poses some tough questions in his "Uncovering Certain Mischievous Questions About the Holocaust," and "Contra the 'Righteous Gentiles.'" Whether one agrees or not with what Lang has to say, one cannot write honestly about the rescuers and avoid the questions he raises. When asking the question "Why didn't more people do what [the rescuers] did?" Lang maintains that the question is posed from a position of moral superiority: "the person asking the question privileges himself: not only should more people have offered such help, but the questioner (we are to suppose) would have been among them."[90] This is neither necessarily the case nor the case in this example. We simply do not know what we would

88. *The Complete Works of Montaigne*, trans. Donald M. Frame (Stanford, Calif.: Stanford University Press, 1958), 819.

89. Primo Levi, *The Drowned and the Saved*, 109, 123–24, 125–26.

90. Lang, "Uncovering Certain Mischievous Questions about the Holocaust," 10.

have done had we been in the place of the rescuers. But this ought not prevent us from determining what we should have done had we been there.

I agree with Lang that the "distinction between Gentiles and non-Gentiles" in the concept and term "Righteous Gentiles" is invidious. I also approve of his striking ethic of "negativity" regarding behavior during the Holocaust that he claims "might indeed be termed obligatory" and which, even if it could not have prevented the genocide, might have obstructed its progress:

> *Not* to volunteer for the voluntary organizations of the Nazi apparatus: the SS, the Einsatzgruppen, the teams of "mercy killers," the Nazi party itself; *not* to take advantage of the opportunistic "windfalls" that occurred as Jews were deported—to take over their businesses or apartments or belongings, to assume their professional positions or practices; *not*, at a farther extreme, to brutalize or to torture—all these varieties of voluntary action could have been avoided without serious risk, almost all of them with no risk whatever. At each of the junctures named, the agents had before them an option of deciding to act by declining to act; that is, to act by inaction. And insofar as the decision for inaction would at these points have required no heroism, would have required only not doing what should not have been done—that was also, we may conclude, what they ought to have done and what could reasonably have been expected of them.[91]

Lang thereby identifies a new category of persons, whom he deems "righteous," who inhabit a middle ground between the rescuers and those who did nothing to help the Jews. These people did not risk their lives to save Jews but they acted, by inaction, in ways that, however slight, made a difference in the process of the Shoah.

At stake here too is the significance of the term "righteous," which in Hebrew *(Hasidei Umoth Ha'olam)* is, according to Lang,

91. Ibid., 10, 12; Lang, *The Future of the Holocaust,* 125.

normally attributed to those who act "rightly," who do what is expected of them, who meet their obligations "more fully than is usually the case in the 'crooked timber of mankind' (otherwise there would be no point in mentioning it at all) but [without] doing more than is required of them or anyone else."[92] However, for Lang, the rescuers of Jews during the Holocaust, those who risked their lives to save persecuted people, could never have been expected to do what they did. Lang's view is that the so-called "righteous" were not "righteous" in the normal sense of the term, but rather "heroic" because, instead of simply meeting expectations, they went "beyond the expectations of normal—rightful—moral conduct."[93] The rescuers should be honored, therefore, not because they did what was required or expected of them but precisely because they did what, "by widely accepted moral standards,"[94] could never have been expected of them. What they did, then, was praiseworthy but not obligatory; and particularly praiseworthy because it was not obligatory. By calling them "righteous," in Lang's view, we at once undervalue them and discount others who may not have risked their lives to save Jews but, by virtue of having done everything that might have been expected of them, were perfectly righteous.

Lang does not then believe that one can demand that human beings risk their lives to save other human beings. He insists that "in none of the principal religious or secular moral codes is there a duty of self-sacrifice, of acting heroically."[95] He can find no legal or moral standard that would require us to put our life, much less the lives of our family, in danger to save others. "Jewish law [itself]," Lang concludes, "although with some dissenting opinion, has generally followed Rabbi Akiba's dictum: 'Thy [own] life comes first.'"[96]

I agree that we cannot legislate that individuals risk their lives

92. Lang, *The Future of the Holocaust*, 120.
93. Ibid.
94. Lang, "Uncovering Certain Mischievous Questions About the Holocaust," 11.
95. Ibid.
96. Lang, *The Future of the Holocaust*, 123.

to save others in the sense that, for example, we cannot punish those who did not rescue Jewish people whom they might have rescued during the Holocaust. But it is not always true that the general public does not expect individuals to risk their lives. Whenever it becomes clear, for example, that people have watched a rape or murder that, even at a risk to their personal safety, they might have stopped and did not, there is generally an outcry against such individuals. Also, there are many dissenting opinions to Rabbi Akiba's rule because the precepts we receive from religion ("rescue the oppressed," Isaiah 1:17; "bring the homeless poor into [your] house," Isaiah 58:7; "love your neighbor as yourself," Luke 10:27/ Leviticus 19:18) either allow for no exceptions or simply do not tell us what the exceptions are. The same is also true of such philosophical commands as Kant's categorical imperative, universal injunctions such as those in the works of Levinas, and concepts, such as the "species self," which demand that our actions be predicated upon criteria much more encompassing than our individual personal welfare. My point is not that we should legislate rescuer behavior, but that we should teach what the rescuers did, and encourage others to demand such behavior of themselves. Even if we view the rescuers metaphorically as the *Lamed Vav,* it is essential not to regard them as heroes operating outside our moral sphere. This would run the risk of our becoming passive admirers, bystanders, as it were. By envisioning the rescuers of Jews during the Holocaust as ordinary people like ourselves, we allow them to bequeath to us their greatest gift: the ability to see ourselves as beings capable of rescue.

The medal given to rescuers by Yad Vashem is inscribed with the Talmudic saying "Whoever saves a single life is as one who has saved an entire world." The rescuers have earned this praise because they rescued not only the Jews but also the concept of the human being as a being capable of self-transcendence even in the most desperate situation and against the most improbable odds. Rescuers risked their lives to save other lives and their acts of goodness were clearly acts of strength. At a time of almost complete moral collapse, they stood their ground, acted according to their consciences, and exhibited the highest possible form of human freedom and responsibility by assuming responsibility for that which most people would not have held them responsible.

Recognizing pure altruism as a foundational motivation is tantamount to seeing it as a nutriment for human beings. It would be a tragic mistake to see such self-transcendence as "self-less" behavior, as some form of self-abnegation or as something that contributes to the depletion of the self. On this point, the testimony of the rescuers is clear and unequivocal. The wonderful paradox that one discovers in reading and listening to the rescuers is that so many of them came to realize, long after having performed their courageous deeds, that their altruistic activities enabled them to reach their highest human potential. Malka Drucker remarks that most of those she interviewed "possessed an enviable peace with themselves" and notes that, for many of them, "the war was their moment of glory: never had right and wrong been so obvious, their reason for living so clear, and never again would they have such an important task before them."[97] André Trocmé writes that he and Magda were never happier than during those years of rescue in Le Chambon-sur-Lignon, and Michel Dreyfus writes about his mother: "When she evoked this entire period, despite the horrors that she underwent and those that she witnessed in prisons and in camps, what prevailed over all other feelings was the profound joy granted her by the awareness of her ability to transcend herself."[98] Madeleine's "profound joy" demonstrates that self-transcendence has nothing to do with self-sacrifice and everything to do with self-fulfillment.

Perhaps more illuminating still is the fact that this pure altru-

97. Gay Block and Malka Drucker, "Introduction," *Rescuers*, 14–15.
98. André Trocmé, "Mémoires," 311. E-mail from Michel Dreyfus (August 22, 2001).

ism can act as a nutriment for its recipient as well as for the doer. According to Primo Levi, what was signified by the act of self-transcendence, rather than the material gift given, was what saved his life in Auschwitz. Levi says of the nightly soup that his Italian laborer friend, Lorenzo, brought to him: "I believe that it was really due to Lorenzo that I am alive today; and not so much for his material aid, as for his having constantly reminded me by his presence, by his natural and plain manner of being good, that there still existed a just world outside our own, something and someone still pure and whole, not corrupt, not savage, extraneous to hatred and terror; something difficult to define, a remote possibility of good, but for which it was worth surviving. . . . Thanks to Lorenzo, I managed not to forget that I myself was a man."[99]

99. Primo Levi, *Survival in Auschwitz* (New York: Macmillan, 1993), 121–22.

Bibliography

"Aggressions Racistes." *Libération,* July 9, 2004, 2.

Arendt, Hannah. *Eichmann in Jerusalem: A Report on the Banality of Evil.* New York: Penguin, 1963.

Arnon, Chana. "Introduction: Jews Rescued Jews During The Holocaust" (unpublished typescript).

Bader, Michael. "Looking a Gift Horse in the Mouth." *Tikkun* 13 (1998): 13–15.

Barnett, Barbara. "Interview with Gérard Bollon." July 1993 (unpublished typescript).

———. "Interview with Marianne Fayol." July 1994 (unpublished typescript).

Baron, Lawrence. "Parochialism, Patriotism, and Philo-Semitism: Why Members of the Reformed Churches Rescued Jews in the Netherlands during the Holocaust." Paper presented at the 28th annual Scholars' Conference on the Holocaust and the Churches (Seattle, 1988).

———. "The Dutchness of Dutch Rescuers: The National Dimension of Altruism." In *Embracing the Other: Philosophical, Psychological, and Historical Perspectives,* edited by Pearl Oliner et al. New York: New York University Press, 1992.

———. "Teaching about the New Psychosocial Research on Rescuers in Holocaust Courses." In *Lessons and Legacies II: Teaching the Holocaust in a Changing World,* edited by Donald G. Schilling, 131–39. Evanston, Ill.: Northwestern University Press, 1998.

Bauer, Yehuda. *Rethinking the Holocaust.* New Haven, Conn.: Yale University Press, 2001.

Bauman, Zygmunt. "The Holocaust's Life as a Ghost." *Tikkun* 13 (1998): 33–38.

Belot, Robert. *Aux frontières de la liberté.* Paris: Fayard, 1998.

Bernard, Serge. "Territoire et marquage identitaire, haut Vivarais et haut Velay." In Cabanel and Gervereau, *La Deuxième Guerre mondiale,* 95–105.

Bibliography

———. "La Construction de la mémoire légendaire au Chambon-sur-Lignon. Mise en scène et reconstitution de l'histoire." Master's thesis, Université Paris 7, Jussieu, 2000.

Besson, Daniel. "Les Assemblées des Frères, darbystes et ravinistes, et l'accueil des Juifs." In Bolle et al., *Le Plateau Vivarais-Lignon*, 86–89.

Bettex, André. "Témoignage d'un ancien Pasteur." In Bolle et al., *Le Plateau Vivarais-Lignon*, 68–71.

Bialik, Hayim Nahman, and Yehoshua Hana Ravnitzky, eds. *The Book of Legends: Legends from the Talmud and Midrash.* New York: Schocken Books, 1992.

Biermann, Wolf. "Epilogue." In *The Pianist*, by Wladyslaw Szpilman. New York: Picador, 1999.

Birnstiel, Eckart, and Chrystel Bernat, eds. *La Diaspora des Huguenots: les réfugiés protestants de France et leur dispersion dans le monde (16e–18e siècles).* Paris: Champion, 2001.

Block, Gay, and Malka Drucker. *Rescuers: Portraits of Moral Courage in the Holocaust.* New York: Holmes & Meier Publishers, 1992.

Blumenthal, David R. *The Banality of Good and Evil: Moral Lessons from the Shoah and Jewish Tradition.* Washington, D.C.: Georgetown University Press, 1999.

Bolle, Pierre, et al., eds. *Le Plateau Vivarais-Lignon: Accueil et Résistance 1939–1944.* Le Chambon-sur-Lignon: Société d'Histoire de la Montagne, 1992.

Bollon, Gérard. "Contribution à l'histoire du Chambon-sur-Lignon: Le Foyer Universitaire des Roches et la rafle de 1943." *Cahiers de la Haute-Loire* (1996): 391–421.

———. *Les séjours d'Albert Camus sur le plateau Vellave (1942–1952).* Saint-Jeures: L'Atelier du Moulin, 2006.

———. "La tradition d'accueil avant la guerre." In Bolle et al., *Le Plateau Vivarais-Lignon*, 151–60.

Boulet, François. "L'attitude spirituelle des protestants devant les Juifs réfugiés." In Bolle et al., *Le Plateau Vivarais-Lignon*, 401–28.

———. "Les prédications des pasteurs." In Bolle et al., *Le Plateau Vivarais-Lignon*, 356–73.

———. "Quelques éléments statistiques." In Bolle et al., *Le Plateau Vivarais-Lignon*, 286–98.

Brog, Mooli. "Yad Vashem." In *The Holocaust Encyclopedia*, edited by Walter Laqueur, 697–701. New Haven, Conn.: Yale University Press, 2001.

Burns, Michael. *Dreyfus, a Family Affair: From the French Revolution to the Holocaust.* New York: Harper Collins, 1991.

Burrin, Philippe. *France under the Germans: Collaboration and Compromise.* Translated by Janet Lloyd. New York: The New Press, 1996.

Buruma, Ian. "The Vichy Syndrome." *Tikkun* 10 (1995): 44–50.

Cabanel, Patrick, and Laurent Gervereau, eds. *La Deuxième Guerre mondiale, des terres de refuge aux musées.* Le Chambon-sur-Lignon: Sivom Vivarais-Lignon, 2003.

Cabanel, Patrick. "L'Israël des Cévennes, réflexions sur une «exception huguenote» face aux juifs." In Cabanel and Gervereau, *La Deuxième Guerre mondiale,* 207–22.

Camus, Albert. *The Plague.* New York: Modern Library, 1948.

———. *Carnets.* May 1935–February 1942. Paris: Gallimard, 1962.

———. *Théâtre, Récits, Nouvelles.* Edited by Roger Quilliot. Paris: Gallimard, Bibliothèque de la Pléiade, 1962.

———. *Carnets.* January 1942–March 1951. Paris: Gallimard, 1964.

———. *Essais.* Edited by Roger Quilliot and Louis Faucon. Paris: Gallimard, Bibliothèque de la Pléiade, 1965.

Camus, Albert, and Pascal Pia. *Correspondance 1939–1947.* Edited by Yves Marc Ajchenbaum. Paris: Fayard/Gallimard, 2000.

Caritey, Aline. "Un chef local: Léon Eyraud." In Bolle et al., *Le Plateau Vivarais-Lignon,* 493–95.

Carroll, James. *Constantine's Sword. The Church and the Jews: A History.* New York: Houghton Mifflin Company, 2001.

Chave, Léon. "Eléments de chronologie." In Bolle et al., *Le Plateau Vivarais-Lignon,* 90–109.

"Chirac: l'antisémitisme 'n'a pas sa place en France.'" *France-Amérique,* January 29–February 4, 2005, 11.

Chouraqui, André. *L'Amour fort comme la mort.* Paris: Editions Robert Laffont, 1990.

Cohen, Rich. *The Avengers.* New York: Alfred Knopf, 2000.

Cole, Tim. *Selling the Holocaust: From Auschwitz to Schindler.* New York: Routledge, 2000.

Coles, Robert. *The Moral Intelligence of Children.* New York: Random House, 1997.

Curtet, Daniel. "Témoignage d'un ancien Pasteur." In Bolle et al., *Le Plateau Vivarais-Lignon,* 54–67.

d'Aubigné, Jeanne Merle. "Souvenirs de quelques camps en France, 1940–1947." In "Quelques Actions des Protestants de France en faveur des Juifs persécutés sous l'Occupation Allemande 1940–1944," edited by Violette Mouchon, 28–66. Paris: La Cimade (unpublished).

Davis, Annette. "Ma mère" (unpublished typescript).

Debiève, Roger. *Mémoires meurtries, mémoire trahie.* Paris: L'Harmattan, 1995.

Dlugoborski, Waclaw, and Franciszek Piper, eds. *Auschwitz 1940–1945: Central Issues in the History of the Camp.* 5 vols. Translated by William Brand. Oswiecim: Auschwitz-Birkenau State Museum, 2000.

Bibliography

Dreyfus, Madeleine. "Extraits d'un témoignage: l'histoire que j'ai vécue d'Octobre 1941 à la Libération—Lyon—Le Chambon-sur-Lignon." Paris: Archives O.S.E., December 1983 (unpublished typescript).

————. "L'O.S.E." In Bolle et al., *Le Plateau Vivarais-Lignon*, 216–19.

————. "Problèmes psycho-sociologiques concernant les camps de déportés" (unpublished typescript).

Dreyfus, Michel. "Un portrait de ma mère" (unpublished typescript).

Dreyfus, Raymond. "Ecoute: une 'psy' selon Alfred Adler" (unpublished).

————. "Mes Souvenirs du Chambon-sur-Lignon au cours des années 1943–44" (unpublished typescript).

Dubois, Henri. "Les communautés catholiques du Plateau." In Bolle et al., *Le Plateau Vivarais-Lignon*, 82–85.

Edelheit, Abraham J., and Hershel Edelheit. *History of the Holocaust: A Handbook and Dictionary.* San Francisco: Westview Press, 1994.

Emmanuel, Pierre. *La Liberté guide nos pas.* Paris: Seghers, 1946.

Fabréguet, Michel. "Les réfugiés et l'accueil." In Bolle et al., *Le Plateau Vivarais-Lignon*, 129–50.

Fayol, Pierre. "Formes de Résistance armée sur le Plateau." In Bolle et al., *Le Plateau Vivarais-Lignon*, 467–74.

————. *Le Chambon-sur-Lignon sous l'occupation (1940–1944).* Paris: L'Harmattan, 1990.

————. *Les Deux France 1936–1945.* Paris: L'Harmattan, 1994.

Fischel, Jack R. *Historical Dictionary of the Holocaust.* Lanham, Md.: Scarecrow Press, 1999.

Fogelman, Eva. *Conscience and Courage: The Rescuers of Jews during the Holocaust.* New York: Doubleday, 1994.

Gabel, Peter. "The Meaning of the Holocaust: Social Alienation and the Infliction of Human Suffering." *Tikkun* 13 (1998): 12–18.

Genestar, Alain. "Casser la figure au racisme." *Paris Match,* July 2004, 23.

Gilbert, Martin. *The Righteous: The Unsung Heroes of the Holocaust.* New York: Henry Holt and Company, 2003.

Gildea, Robert. *Marianne in Chains: Daily Life in the Heart of France During the German Occupation.* New York: Henry Holt and Company, 2002.

Golsan, Richard J., ed. *Memory, The Holocaust, and French Justice: The Bousquet and Touvier Affairs.* Hanover, N.H.: University Press of New England, 1996.

Gordan, Bertram M. *Historical Dictionary of World War II France: The Occupation, Vichy, and the Resistance, 1938–1946.* Westport, Conn.: Greenwood Press, 1998.

Gossels, Lisa. *The Children of Chabannes.* New York: Perennial Pictures, 2000.

Grob, Leonard. "Rescue during the Holocaust—and Today." *Judaism* 46 (1997): 98–107.

Gushee, David P. *The Righteous Gentiles of the Holocaust: A Christian Inter-pretation.* Minneapolis, Minn.: Fortress Press, 1994.

Gutman, Israel. Editor in chief. *Encyclopedia of the Holocaust.* New York: Macmillan Publishing Company, 1990.

Hallie, Philip. *The Scar of Montaigne.* Middletown, Conn.: Wesleyan University Press, 1966.

———. "The Ethics of Montaigne's 'De la cruauté.'" In *O un Amy! Essays on Montaigne in Honor of Donald M. Frame,* edited by Raymond La Charité, 156–71. Lexington, Ky.: French Forum, 1977.

———. *Lest Innocent Blood Be Shed: The Story of the Village of Le Chambon and How Goodness Happened There.* New York: Harper & Row, 1994.

———. "Camus's Hug." *The American Scholar* 64 (1995): 428–35.

Hatzfeld, Olivier. "L'Ecole Nouvelle Cévenole: nouvelle approche." In Bolle et al., *Le Plateau Vivarais-Lignon,* 161–74.

Henry, Patrick, ed. *Approaches to Teaching Montaigne's "Essays."* New York: Modern Language Association of America, 1994.

Houssel, Jean-Pierre. "La résistance civile sur le Plateau: paysans et pa-triotes." In Cabanel and Gervereau, *La Deuxième Guerre mondiale,* 107–16.

Isenberg, Sheila. *A Hero of Our Own: The Story of Varian Fry.* New York: Random House, 2001.

Jackson, Julian. *France: The Dark Years 1940–1944.* New York: Oxford University Press, 2001.

"Jacques Chirac en terre d'accueil et de refuge." *L'Eveil* (de la Haute Loire), July 9, 2004, 10.

Judt, Tony. "On *The Plague.*" *The New York Review of Books,* November 29, 2001, 6–9.

Kauffmann, Stanley. "A Bouquet of Lives." *The New Republic,* June 9, 2003, 24–25.

Kieval, Hillel J. "Legality and Resistance in Vichy France: The Rescue of Jewish Children." *Proceedings of the American Philosophical Society* 124 (October 1980): 339–66.

Klarsfeld, Serge. *French Children of the Holocaust: A Memorial.* New York: New York University Press, 1996.

Knout, David. *Contribution à l'histoire de la Résistance Juive en France 1940–1944.* Paris: Editions du Centre, 1947.

Lang, Berel. *The Future of the Holocaust: Between History and Memory.* Ithaca, N.Y.: Cornell University Press, 1999.

———. "Uncovering Certain Mischievous Questions about the Holo-caust." Ina Levine Scholar-in-Residence Annual Lecture. Washington, D.C.: United States Holocaust Memorial Museum, 2002.

Langer, Lawrence. *Admitting the Holocaust.* New York: Oxford University Press, 1995.

Bibliography

Latour, Anny. *La Résistance juive en France (1940–1944)*. Paris: Stock, 1970.

Lazare, Lucien. *Le Livre des Justes*. Paris: Editions Jean-Claude Lattès, 1993.

———. *Rescue as Resistance: How Jewish Organizations Fought the Holocaust in France*. Translated by Jeffrey M. Green. New York: Columbia University Press, 1996.

———, ed. *Dictionnaire des Justes de France*. Paris: Fayard, 2003.

Lemalet, Martine, ed. *Au secours des enfants du siècle. Regards croisés sur l'O.S.E*. Paris: Nil Editions, 1993.

Levi, Primo. "Afterword." *The Reawakening*. New York: Simon & Schuster, 1965.

———. *The Drowned and the Saved*. New York: Random House, 1988.

———. *Survival in Auschwitz*. New York: Macmillan, 1993.

Lifton, R. J. *The Future of Immortality and Other Essays for a Nuclear Age*. New York: Basic Books, 1987.

Lottman, Herbert R. *Albert Camus: A Biography*. Garden City, N.Y.: Doubleday, 1979.

MacMillan, Ian. *Village of a Million Spirits*. Hanover, N.H.: Steerforth Press, 1999.

Marrus, Michael R., and Robert O. Paxton. *Vichy France and the Jews*. Stanford, Calif.: Stanford University Press, 1981.

McCarthy, Patrick. *Camus: A Critical Study of His Life and Work*. London: Hamish Hamilton, 1982.

Menut, Georges. "André Trocmé: un violent vaincu par Dieu." In Bolle et al., *Le Plateau Vivarais-Lignon*, 378–400.

———. *Le Chambon-sur-Lignon: un village pas comme les autres*. Le Chambon-sur-Lignon: Société d'Histoire de la Montagne, 1995.

Metzger, Bruce M., and Michael D. Coogan, eds. *The Oxford Companion to the Bible*. New York: Oxford University Press, 1993.

Monroe, Kristen Renwick. *The Heart of Altruism: Perceptions of a Common Humanity*. Princeton, N.J.: Princeton University Press, 1996.

———. *The Hand of Compassion: Portraits of Moral Choice during the Holocaust*. Princeton, N.J.: Princeton University Press, 2004.

Moore, Deborah Dash. *GI Jews: How World War II Changed a Generation*. Cambridge, Mass.: Harvard University Press, 2004.

Niewyk, Donald, and Francis Nicosia. *The Columbia Guide to the Holocaust*. New York: Columbia University Press, 2000.

Nossiter, Adam. *The Algeria Hotel: France, Memory and the Second World War*. New York: Houghton Mifflin, 2001.

Novick, Peter. *The Holocaust in American Life*. New York: Houghton Mifflin, 1999.

Oliner, Samuel P., and Pearl M. Oliner. *The Altruistic Personality: Rescuers of Jews in Nazi Europe.* New York: The Free Press, 1988.

Ousby, Ian. *Occupation: The Ordeal of France 1940–1944.* New York: St. Martin's Press, 1998.

Ozick, Cynthia. "Prologue." In Block and Drucker, *Rescuers,* xi–xvi.

———. "Roundtable Discussion." In *Writing and the Holocaust,* edited by Berel Lang, 277–84. New York: Holmes & Meier, 1988.

Paldiel, Mordecai. *Saving the Jews: Amazing Stories of Men and Women Who Defied the "Final Solution."* Rockville, Md.: Schreiber Publishing, 2000.

Paul, Annie Murphy. "Born to be Good?" *USA Weekend,* July 23–25, 1999, 6.

Paxton, Robert O. *Vichy France: Old Guard and New Order, 1940–1944.* New York: Columbia University Press, 1972.

Picon, Gaëtan. "Notes on *The Plague.*" In *Camus, A Collection of Critical Essays,* edited by Germaine Brée, 145–51. Englewood Cliffs, N.J.: Prentice-Hall, 1962.

Plazas, Antonio. "Remarques concernant les listes du registre de 'La Maison des Roches.'" In Bolle et al., *Le Plateau Vivarais-Lignon,* 635–38.

Poujol, Jacques. "Les Victimes." In Bolle et al., *Le Plateau Vivarais-Lignon,* 639–47.

———. *Protestants dans la France en guerre 1939–1945. Dictionnaire thématique et biographique.* Paris: Les Editions de Paris, 2000.

Poznanski, Renée. *Les Juifs en France pendant la Seconde Guerre mondiale.* Paris: Hachette, 1994.

Quilliot, Roger. *The Sea and Prisons: A Commentary on the Life and Thought of Albert Camus.* Translated by Emmett Parker. University: University of Alabama Press, 1970.

Rittner, Carol, and Sondra Myers, eds. *The Courage to Care: Rescuers of Jews during the Holocaust.* New York: New York University Press, 1986.

Rochat, François, and André Modigliani. "The Ordinary Quality of Resistance: From Milgram's Laboratory to the Village of Le Chambon." *Journal of Social Issues* 51 (1995): 195–212.

Rosowsky, Oscar. "Les faux papiers d'identité au Chambon-sur-Lignon 1942–1944." In Bolle et al., *Le Plateau Vivarais-Lignon,* 232–61.

Samuel, Vivette. *Sauver les enfants.* Paris: Liana Levi, 1995.

Sauvage, Pierre. *Weapons of the Spirit.* Los Angeles: Le Chambon Foundation, 1989.

Schulweis, Harold M. *For Those Who Can't Believe: Overcoming the Obstacles to Faith.* New York: Harper Collins, 1994.

Senesh, Hannah. *Hannah Senesh: Her Life and Diary.* New York: Schocken Books, 1972.

Bibliography

Silberman, Brian. *Manifest.* Tampa, Fla.: University of Tampa, 2003.

Smith, Craig S. "Thwarted in Germany, Neo-Nazis Take Fascism to France." *New York Times,* August 13, 2004, A3.

Tec, Nechama. *When Light Pierced the Darkness: Christian Rescue of Jews in Nazi-Occupied Poland.* New York: Oxford University Press, 1986.

———. "Helping Behavior and Rescue during the Holocaust." In *Lessons and Legacies: The Meaning of the Holocaust in a Changing World,* edited by Peter Hayes, 210–24. Evanston, Ill.: Northwestern University Press, 1991.

———. "Righteous Among the Nations." In Laqueur, *The Holocaust Encyclopedia,* 569–74.

Theis, Edouard, and André Trocmé. "Message des deux pasteurs du Chambon à leur paroisse." In Bolle et al., *Le Plateau Vivarais-Lignon,* 597–99.

Thibaud, Paul. "La Culpabilité française." *Esprit* 168 (1991): 23–30.

———. "La République et ses héros: Le Gaullisme pendant et après la guerre." *Esprit* 198 (1994): 64–83.

———. "Un temps de mémoire." *Le Débat* 96 (1996): 166–83.

Todd, Olivier. *Albert Camus, une vie.* Paris: Gallimard, 1996.

Todorov, Tzvetan. *Face à l'extrême.* Paris: Editions du Seuil, 1991.

Trocmé, André. "Mémoires." Peace Collection at the Swarthmore College Library (unpublished).

Trocmé, Charles. "Daniel Geoffroy Trocmé (1912–1944)" (unpublished typescript).

Trocmé, Magda. "Le Chambon." In Rittner and Myers, *The Courage to Care,* 100–107.

Trocmé, Magda, Madeleine Barot, Pierre Fayol, O. Rosowsky. "Le Mythe du commandant SS protecteur des Juifs." *Le Monde Juif,* April–June 1988, 61–69.

Trocmé Grilli di Cortona, Magda. "Souvenirs Autobiographiques." Peace Collection at the Swarthmore College Library (unpublished).

Van Ruymbeke, Bertrand, and Randy J. Sparks, eds. *Memory and Identity: The Huguenots in France and the Atlantic Diaspora.* Columbia: University of South Carolina Press, 2003.

Wajda, Andrzej. *Korczak.* Warsaw: Studio Filmowe "Perspektwa," 1990.

Waltzer, Kenneth. "Jewish Underground and the Rescue of Jews in Poland." Paper presented at the 35th annual Scholars' Conference on the Holocaust and the Churches (Philadelphia, March 8, 2005).

Weber, Eugen. "France's Downfall." *The Atlantic Monthly,* October 2001, 117–24.

Weightman, John. "The Outsider." *The New York Review of Books,* January 15, 1998, 26–29.

Weisberg, Richard. *Vichy Law and the Holocaust in France.* New York: New York University Press, 1996.

Zeitoun, Sabine. "Accueil d'enfants Juifs de l'Oeuvre de Secours aux Enfants (O.S.E.) par le Plateau Vivarais-Lignon." In Bolle et al., *Le Plateau Vivarais-Lignon,* 221–26.

———. *Ces enfants qu'il fallait sauver.* Paris: Albin Michel, 1989.

———. *L'Oeuvre de Secours aux Enfants (O.S.E.) sous l'Occupation en France.* Paris: L'Harmattan, 1990.

Zuccotti, Susan. *The Holocaust, the French, and the Jews.* New York: Harper Collins, 1993.

Index

Index

Bouix, Jean (rescuer), 109–10, 112, 130
Boulet, François, 123, 124
Boy Scouts, as rescuers, 10, 88, 91
Breton, André: rescue of, 146
British Army: Jewish Brigade in, 87
Brottes, Marie (rescuer), 36, 102, 152
brown plague. *See* Occupation, German
Brückberger, Raymond-Léopold, 109, 110
Buchenwald concentration camp: children of, 95; Jewish resistance in, 84–85
Bulgaria: Jewish resistance in, 11, 85
Burrin, Philippe, 4, 5, 15
bystanders, 13, 159, 162, 166, 168. *See also* passivity

Cabanel, Patrick, 27–28
Caligula (Camus), 110
Calvin, Jean: sympathy for Jews, 28, 151, 152
Camus, Albert: *Caligula,* 110; feelings of exile, 113–14; in French Resistance, 112–13, 127; illness of, 106, 107, 113, 115–16, 129, 133; *Letters to a German Friend,* 108; *The Misunderstanding,* 110; *The Myth of Sisyphus,* 108; on nonviolence, 127–28; *Notebooks,* 105, 107, 113, 114, 115, 116, 117, 118, 123, 134, 135; *The Plague,* 105–36; *The Rebel,* 105; *The Stranger,* 108, 115; on Vivarais-Lignon plateau, xiii, 105–6, 108, 109, 111, 112, 114, 118, 120, 129–30, 133, 136; work with French Resistance, 112–13
Camus, Francine (wife of Albert), 106, 112
caring, as motivating factor, 148, 153
Catholics, 37; anti-Semitism of, 150; Italian, 152; protests by, 15; as rescuers, 10, 92, 154; silence of, 13
Chagall, Marc: rescue of, 145
Chagrin et la pitié, Le (documentary), 2
Chaillet, Father Pierre (rescuer), 92
Chalmers, Burns (rescuer), 19, 33–34
Chambonisation, 7
character, as motivating factor, 149–50
Chazot, M. and Mme Ernest, 19
Chevrier, Félix (rescuer), 102

children: deaths of, 126–27; deportation of, 14, 88–89; education of, 24, 38, 45–46; evacuation from concentration camps, 33–34, 45, 87, 89–90, 117; houses of refuge for, 29, 45–46; raising of altruistic, 147–48, 153, 155, 163; rescue of, 16, 75, 102; of rescuers, 97–98; sheltering of, 6, 18–20, 29–30, 68–72, 85, 87–93, 111, 132
Children of Chabannes, The (documentary), 90, 102
Children's Rescue Network. *See* Oeuvre de secours aux enfants
Chirac, Jacques, xx–xxii, 61
Chouraqui, André (rescuer), 73, 110–11, 112, 113, 117, 129
Christians: failure to help the Jews, 11, 13, 101; Nazism opposed to, xix, 125; pacifist, xix, 21, 37-38; in *The Plague,* 123; protests by, 16; as rescuers of Jews, 11, 13, 32, 101–3, 139, 142–44, 151–52; resistance by, xix; Social, 123. *See also individual denominations*
Christophe, Marcelle (survivor), 94
churches: silence of, 11, 13. *See also specific religions*
cities of refuge, 34–35, 39. *See also* houses of refuge
cohabitation. *See* accommodation/ accommodators
Coles, Robert, 163
collaboration/collaborators, 146; active, 11–13, 42, 122, 123, 125; myths regarding, 2–5; resistance to, 5, 87
Combat (Resistance newspaper), 108
Comité de la rue Amelot, Le (Amelot Street Group), 87
communications networks, 23
Communists, 2, 42; sheltering of, 25
community, sense of: as motivating factor, 121, 154–55; in *The Plague,* 115–16
compassion, as motivating factor, 99, 144, 148, 151, 156, 159, 162, 163
competence, as motivating factor, 148
Compulsory Labor Service (Service du travail obligatoire, STO), 15, 25

Index

Index

65, 68–72, 77, 94, 95–96; population of, 16; Protestants in, 27–29,
36; rescue missions in, 6–11, 16,
18–27, 30, 102, 124; rescuers in,
140, 155–56; resistance activity
in, 110, 112–13, 129–34; shelter-
ing children in, 68–72, 117; tour-
ism in, 31–32
Lederman, Charles (rescuer), 92
Le Forestier, Roger, 46, 129
Les Grillons (house of refuge), 46,
53–55
Lest Innocent Blood Be Shed (Hallie), xii,
6–8, 18–20, 131
Letters to a German Friend (Camus),
108
Levi, Primo, 83, 84, 118, 165, 170
Levinas, Emmanuel, 99, 168
Leviticus (Bible): 19.18, 99–100, 168;
19.34, 100
Lévy, Madeleine Dreyfus (Resistance
fighter), 65n2
Leynaud, René, 108–9, 129
Lifton, Robert, 160
Lipchitz, Jacques: rescue of, 145
Lithuania: Baptists in, 151; ghettos
in, 82
Loewenstein, Hermann (deported),
48n5
Loinger, Georges (rescuer), 90, 91
Loire Valley. *See* Haute-Loire
loss, personal, as motivating factor,
148, 156
Lottman, Herbert, 109, 110, 112, 118
Louis XIV (king of France), 27
love, 144; for God, 100; for neighbors,
35–36, 99–101, 102, 120, 151,
168; pure, 161n81; between sepa-
rated people, 115
Lublin, Lucien (Jewish resistance
fighter), 86
Luke (Bible): 10.25–37, 35–36, 100,
168
Luther, Martin: anti-Semitism of, 28
Lutheran Church: in Denmark, 151; in
Germany, 152
Lvov ghetto, 84
Lyon: French Resistance in, 108,
129–30
Lyon–Le Chambon-sur-Lignon escape

route, 65, 68–71. *See also* Garel
Network
Lys, Daniel, 123

Maber, Gladys Lesley (rescuer), 19
McCarthy, Patrick, 109, 110
Maidanek concentration camp, xiii, 48,
57, 140; Jewish resistance in, 84
Mairesse, Simon (rescuer), 70
Maison des Roches, La (house of ref-
uge), 45–46, 49, 55–57; roundup
at, 47–48, 63
Malle, Louis, 3
maquis (underground), 42, 86–87, 88,
131–32. *See also* French Resis-
tance; underground, Jewish
Marchandeau Law (1940), 12–13
marginality: of Jews, 13, 16; as moti-
vating factor, 146–47; of Protes-
tants, 27; of rescuers, 154–55
Marianne in Chains (Gildea), 4, 5
Marion, Mlle and Mme (rescuers), 19
Mark (Bible): 12.28–34, 100
Martin-Cayre, Sérafin (survivor), 48n5
Martin-Lopez, Félix (survivor), 48n5
Marx, Georges (victim), 48
Masour, Germaine (rescuer), 76, 96
Matthew (Bible): 22.34-40, 100
Maus (Spiegelman), 139
Melville, Jean-Pierre, 2
"Mémoires" (André Trocmé), 18–20,
22, 42, 46, 47, 57, 126, 131–32
Menut, Georges, 20–21, 23, 39, 124
Michel, Henri, 2
Miles Lerman Center for the Study of
Jewish Resistance, 93n26
Misunderstanding, The (Camus), 110
Modiano, Patrick, 3
Monbrison, Françoise de, 37
money, as motivating factor, 31–32,
146
Monroe, Kristen, 148–49, 153, 154,
156
Montaigne, Michel, xi, 164–65
Moral Intelligence of Children, The
(Coles), 163
morality: ambiguous, 5; elevated, 31,
32, 159, 161n81, 167; human, 99;
in *The Plague*, 116, 119–20. *See
also* courage, moral; ethics

Index

Moral-Lopez, Pedro (survivor), 48n5
Moulin, Jean (Resistance leader), 2
Mouvement de jeunesse sioniste (MJS), 88, 91
museums of the Holocaust, 8, 93n26. *See also* Yad Vashem
Muslims: racism against, xx–xxi
Myth of Sisyphus, The (Camus), 108

narcissism, as motivating factor, 161–62
Nazis: anti-Christian doctrine of, xix, 125; anti-Semitism of, 124; brutality of, 82–83, 144, 165; collaboration with, 2–5, 11–13, 42, 87, 125, 146; Jewish resistance against, 82, 86–87; reprisals by, 93, 132; resistance against, 8, 21, 30, 42, 105–6, 116, 123, 129–36, 151. *See also* Gestapo; Holocaust
needy, help for, as motivating factor, 146–48, 153, 162, 163, 168. *See also* altruism
negativity, ethic of, 166
neighbors: love for, 35–36, 99–101, 102, 120, 151, 168
Netherlands, the. *See* Holland
Niemöller, Martin (pastor), 21
nonbelievers, as rescuers, 10–11, 38, 92, 133. *See also* gentiles
nonintervention, attitude of, 136. *See also* inaction
nonrescuers, 155–56, 166
nonviolence, 6, 126; Camus on, 127–28; Christian, 7n9; on Vivarais-Lignon plateau, 18, 36–38, 40. *See also* pacifism
nonviolent resistance, xiii, 8, 21, 42; Jewish, 83–84, 87–93; in Le Chambon-sur-Lignon, 105–6, 113; on Vivarais-Lignon plateau, 129–36. *See also* rescue missions
North Africa: Allied invasion of, 106, 113, 115; Jewish resistance in, 86
Nossiter, Adam, 132
Notebooks (Camus), 105; notes on *The Plague* in, 114, 116, 117, 118, 134, 135; quotations from, 107, 113, 115, 123
Novick, Peter, 158

Numbers (Bible): 35.9-31, 34
Nuremberg Laws (1935), 12

obedience, as motivating factor, 155–56
Occupation, German: French reaction to, 1–6; heroism during, 138; 1942 changes in, 15–16; *The Plague* as allegory, 114–16, 126, 130, 133–34; rescues during, 8–12, 43; resistance to, 131; sermons during, 122, 123–27
Occupied Zone: Jews defined in, 12–13; life in, 105; resistance in, 87, 131–32, 136; roundups in, 14, 46. *See also* Unoccupied Zone
Oeuvre de secours aux enfants (Children's Rescue Network, OSE): Madeleine Dreyfus' work for, 65, 68–72, 93, 95, 96; rescue of children by, 10, 32–33, 87, 89–92, 111, 117
Old Testament, 102. *See also* Hebrew Bible
Oliner, Pearl M. and Samuel P., 147, 149, 151, 153, 154, 155, 156, 160
Ophüls, Marcel, 2
Ophüls, Max, rescue of, 145–46
opportunistic accommodation, 4. *See also* collaboration/collaborators
OSE. *See* Oeuvre de secours aux enfants
Oullins, M. and Mme Paul Jouve d' (rescuers), 68
Ousby, Ian, 6
Ozick, Cynthia, 140, 144, 163

pacifism, 18, 42, 123, 134–35; Christian, 21, 36–37, 151
Paldiel, Mordecai, 98–99
Panelier; Camus in, 106, 108, 111, 112, 114, 118, 133, 136
parents, as motivating factor, 147–48, 153, 155, 163
Paris: liberation of, 86
partisans, Jewish, 85, 86–87, 131
passivity, 136, 166; avoidance of, xxi, 158–59; French, 2–5; Jewish, xiii, 81–82, 93. *See also* bystanders
pastors, on Vivarais-Lignon plateau, 21, 24–25, 35, 68–69, 92, 123

Index

Index

Unitarian Service Committee, 88, 89, 91
United States: failure to rescue Jews, 85; pacifism in, 36; support for rescuers in, 144
unity. *See* solidarity
universalistic principles, 153
Unoccupied Zone: houses of refuge in, 90; roundups in, 13–14, 46, 91–92. *See also* Occupied Zone
Unsworth, Richard, 19
U.S. Holocaust Memorial Museum, 93n26

vacation camps, 29
Valla, Francis, xxii
values, as motivating factor, 147–50, 153, 156, 162
Vel d'Hiv roundup, 14–15, 30, 87, 117, 123, 124
vengeance, elimination of, 38, 40, 128
Vénissieux Night, 92
Vexin region, 101–2
Vichy France (Paxton), 3
Vichy government: anti-Semitism of, 11–16, 21, 29, 124–25; Catholic support for, 15; collaboration by, 12–13, 122, 123; deportation of Jewish children by, 90; raids by, 45, 47; repression by, 5; resistance to, 21, 25, 42, 86–87, 105–6, 131; scrutiny of, 2–4
victims. *See* dehumanization; Jews; *and individuals by name*
Villasant-Dura, Jules (survivor), 48n5
Vilna ghetto, 84
violence: healing versus, 135; Protestant opposition to, 36–37; useless, 165
violent resistance: Jewish, 84–87, 93; in Le Chambon-sur-Lignon, xiii, 105–6; on Vivarais-Lignon plateau, 8, 131–36. *See also* French Resistance
Vivarais-Lignon plateau, xiii; Camus living on, xiii, 105–6, 108, 109, 111, 112, 114, 118, 120, 129–30, 133, 136; Chirac's visit to, xx–xxii; pacifism of, 36–38, 40, 123; pastors on, 18, 21, 24–25, 35, 68–69, 92, 123; as place of sanctuary, 34–35; in *The Plague*, 118–23; rescue missions on, 6–11, 18–27, 41, 124, 129–30; rescuers on, xx, 40, 119–21, 152; resistance activity, 8, 29–32, 129–36; sermons on, 123–27; tradition of sheltering, 29–32. *See also* Le Chambon-sur-Lignon; Panelier; Saint-Etienne; Tence
Vosquijl, Elizabeth Van (rescuer), 145

Wallenberg, Raoul (rescuer), 145
Waltzer, Ken, 103
War of the Camisards, 37
Warsaw ghetto: orphanage in, 102; uprising in, 84
Weapons of the Spirit (documentary), 28, 36, 38, 71, 102, 120, 121, 131, 152
Weber, Eugen, 5
Weightman, John, 130
Weill, Joseph (rescuer), 90, 92
Weiss, Frantz (deported), 48n5
When Light Pierced the Darkness (Tec), 146
Wollstein, Herbert (victim), 48
workers, French: deportations of, 15, 25
works. *See* deeds
World War II: in *The Plague*, 130
Wouters, Camille (deported), 48n5

Yad Vashem, 9, 11, 41–42, 93n26, 141, 143. *See also* Righteous Among the Nations designation
YMCA, 19, 32, 88, 89, 91
Yugoslavia: Jewish partisans in, 85

Zeitoun, Sabine, 22, 93